CUDDLE A MEMORY

How to Survive Losing a Loved One

CAROLYN PUTTNAM

10-10-10
Publishing

Cuddle a Memory, How to Survive Losing a Loved One

www.cuddleamemorybook.com

ISBN-13: 978-1981312863
ISBN-10: 1981312862

Limits of Liability and Disclaimer of Warranty

The author and publisher shall not be liable for your misuse of the enclosed material. This book is strictly for informational and educational purposes only.

Warning – Disclaimer

The purpose of this book is to educate and entertain. The author and/ or publisher do not guarantee that anyone following these techniques, suggestions, tips, ideas, or strategies will become successful. The author and/or publisher shall have neither liability nor responsibility to anyone with respect to any loss or damage caused, or alleged to be caused, directly or indirectly by the information contained in this book.

Medical Disclaimer

The medical or health information in this book is provided as an information resource only, and is not to be used or relied on for any diagnostic or treatment purposes. This information is not intended to be patient education, does not create any patient-physician relationship, and should not be used as a substitute for professional diagnosis and treatment.

Publisher

10-10-10 Publishing
Markham, ON
Canada

Printed in Canada and the United States of America

I would like to dedicate this book to

My Past

My lovely Dad and Grandparents

My Present

My ever-supportive Mum, Brothers and Husband

My Future

My radiant Sweet P

Table of Contents

Acknowledgements

I would like to acknowledge and thank the following:

Bereavement Matters for their help and treatment when I needed it the most, advice for training as a counsellor and encouragement for writing my book. As a gesture of thanks, I pledge to donate five per cent of profit from sales of my book to them.

Deidre Sanders for agreeing to write my foreword; her positive feedback to my book was the confidence boost I needed.

The Counselling Foundation for their training and encouragement towards my new qualifications. Not forgetting my friends from the course, thank you for your support and interest. I promise you have my full attention now.

Raymond Aaron, for being in the right place when I needed guidance, and my book architect, Dyann Olivieira, for her advice and guidance. Both have been invaluable.

All the team at Sainsbury's St Albans, especially Paul Dennison and Lauren Waind, for their support, encouragement and allowing me to be where I needed to.

Carolina Brennan and the team at the Anti-Ageing Clinic, Park Street, and all the lovely clients, for persevering and getting to know me, and putting up with me during the worst time of my life.

Tracy Bengougam for always inspiring, encouraging and

believing in me. I thank you for everything you have ever given me.

All my personal beauty clients who have continually shown their interest, shared their stories with me and given me the chance to grow as a therapist and a person. Particular thanks go to Julia Allam, Judy Harris, Catherine Levick, Alison Martin, Ruth Medina, Julia Robinson, Dawn Russell, Anna Sheriff and Tanya Spencer. They have all taken turns being understanding while I was in tears during treatments and have become my friends.

To all my fabulous friends who, despite my best efforts, stuck by me with love, support and laughter when I needed them and in a way inspired the material for this book. Special mentions to Lisa, Serena, Tina, Wendy, Laura, Leighann, James, Jamie, Jaspal and Ruth.

My adoptive families, the Honeys and the Webbs, for their constant love.

Most importantly, my brilliant family. Mum, because without her help and love this would not have been possible; my husband, Andy, who throughout has been generous with love, time and effort; my brothers, Dave and CJ, for just being them; my sisters-in-law for being above all great friends; and my aunts, cousins and in-laws for being there.

Foreword

Oscar Wilde said death and taxes were the only two things in life we could be sure of, but even though it touches us all, death, the bereavement, sense of loss and grief that follow are all matters we find tremendously difficult to talk about.

People will say they don't know what to say to someone who has suffered a loss, they are afraid of saying the wrong thing, perhaps causing offence or further upset.

Carolyn Puttnam has here drawn upon these feelings of uselessness, of the fear and difficulty we all face talking about death, along with her experiences in the wake of the death of her own father, grandfather and grandmother, all within a year, to help guide the reader through their own troubles.

She tells the reader to allow themselves to feel whatever it is they are feeling – there are no wrong answers and it is OK to feel angry or upset, or indeed anything.

When her own father died, Carolyn wanted a book that would help her. She couldn't find one, so she wrote it herself.

—*Deidre Sanders,*
 Agony Aunt

Introduction

As you are reading this book, you have had the life-changing event and the horrible experience of losing someone you loved or was important to you.

I am sorry for your loss.

It could also be that someone you care about has lost someone, but either way I'm guessing you are here in an attempt to understand what you or they are going through, how to help and try to gain a better understanding of what lies ahead, and how you can cope with it.

My hope for this book is that it will give you something to relate to and help you cope with the grief of losing a loved one.

This is not a book of clinical information or professional advice but of personal experience and is something I desperately wanted to read when I was in your situation. This was not only to help prepare myself; but I wished I could have given the book to those around me – friends, family, work colleagues – so they too could have an understanding of what I was going through in terms of the whirlwind of confusing and contradictory thoughts and feelings.

I needed honest and blunt information at this time, but equally I needed handling very delicately. All the books I could find seemed to be long-winded and full of phrases I just could not find the mental capacity to absorb and work through; I needed a short, succinct book full of real-world advice to help me to try and figure it all out and work through this confusing time.

The ultimate message is that grief is a completely personal thing and everyone will cope – or not cope, it might seem at times – in different ways, and **there is no right or wrong way to grieve.**

My aim is to share my thoughts and feelings as honestly as I can so you do not feel alone, and to say things that no one ever does – well, things that no one ever told me or expressed to me before or during this time.

I have included chapters on what to expect at different times in the aftermath of losing someone; there is a chapter for family, friends and work colleagues to read if they are struggling to relate to what you are experiencing; and a chapter on how different faiths cope with death and grief. Many people believe religion and faith can be a great support, whether it's the process of format and routine or that it helps a person to 'figure out' their loss and serve as a comfort. For some people, death of course makes their religious beliefs stronger; for others, it can shake them so fundamentally as to make them question a lifetime of prior dedication. There can be elements of another religion that resonate with you and help you to cope with mental upheaval.

I have included in the chapter for friends and family to read what I wished I had said to those around me, because while they offered me support, it did not always feel that helpful to me; I think mostly that came from me not being able to acknowledge and articulate what I needed from them. I also did not want to be ungrateful. What I felt at that time is what I now say to others when they have lost someone they care about.

I learned about the Kubler-Ross model, or the five stages of grief – these are: Denial, Anger, Bargaining, Depression and Acceptance. You may well have learned about these yourself, as I did at the beginning of my pain. I rejected the model as I saw the five stages as some sort of checklist, which I was failing to complete; but now I know they are the emotions I was going through. I could have two in two minutes or all five in frantic rotation throughout the day; these constantly changing emotions actually made me feel sick with dizziness as my head was in such turmoil.

A doctor and counsellor each independently told me I could expect it to take between four and 12 months to 'feel better' or recover from a bereavement, but in my opinion that will vary depending on your relationship with that person, their age and to what extent their death was expected. My grandparents were between four to six months before I 'felt better' in any way, but my dad is still an ongoing process six years on.

It is 100% your experience. I only want to try to help prepare you for what might happen based on my family, friends and how I felt in a similar situation.

Some people fall apart and are housebound for weeks or months or more, while others will put the loss in a box to deal with later – that can take years or perhaps never; but I think if you are reading this you are seeking help and are probably going to work through similar experiences to mine. This book is based on my experiences, so there are references to them as examples where I felt they could be useful.

By way of explanation it will probably help if I provide a little of my story as background,, give you an indication of what made me want to write the book, why I felt I might be able to help others and why I feel I have perhaps an idea of some of the things you might be feeling.

My maternal grandfather died suddenly of heart failure when I was 12, in the summer between primary and secondary school.

My paternal grandmother had a relatively non-aggressive form of cancer and her health had slowly been deteriorating for several years after she had suffered a stroke. As a family, we watched her fade from the once-strong, lively lady over many years and she eventually died in a hospice when I was 23.

My father developed Acute Myeloid Leukaemia, he lived for just 62 days after his diagnosis, and his deterioration was extremely fast; he died while my husband and I were still on a plane on our way to see him. I was 32.

My paternal grandfather died four weeks after my father at the grand old age of 97, after he had been ill in hospital for several months. My maternal grandmother died nine months later on New Year's Eve, aged 86. She had been in and out of hospital all year and had suffered poor health for a few years previously, leaving her confused and not herself.

So, the family had three bereavements in 11 months; some we might have expected, some were a shock. Each one was difficult and upsetting, but losing my dad has been particularly hard. However, now, after six years, moving house, having our daughter and my brother's wedding, I finally feel like I am starting to get a handle on it – after the many, many sessions of counselling.

It is not until I went through these three bereavements that I began to realise how little we as a society talk about death and grief. Therefore, no one really knows how to talk about it, deal with it or be around, talk to, or support people who are grieving. I feel it is important to open the subject up and make it easier for everyone. I would like for this book to be some sort of tool to open communication about this dark, depressing but inevitable event.

The bottom line is that grief is a completely personal thing, and everyone will have different times when they feel they are coping or not coping and, again, there is no right or wrong way for you to grieve.

It probably is possible to muddle through on autopilot, and it's OK to do so; but it is also acceptable (and in my view healthy) to say to people: 'This is how I feel and I might not know what to do next. I might like to go and hibernate or go back on autopilot.'

But remember, you are stronger than you think.

CHAPTER 1

Knowing It Is Coming

Bereave: To deprive of a relation, friend etc., especially by death

Whether your loved one has died already or you are in preparation for this sad and difficult time, the period prior to a death becomes part of the experience, whether you realise at the time or not.

If you are preparing mentally, physically and emotionally, then hopefully you will find some ideas to help. Likewise, I hope it will resonate with you if you are picking this book up as a tool to help if you have been bereaved. I also hope it will provide comfort for the pain you already have.

After a person has died, the nature of your relationship and the time you spend in the period leading up to their death will take on a new significance.

Things will happen that will make you relive certain dates and feelings. Perhaps it was noticing the passing of a season, the leaves on the trees changing colour or the first sight of snowdrops that show the signs of a fresh start and new season – maybe it was something your loved one enjoyed. These events now will be heightened as they will attune your memories of the person you are missing, and you will remember the last time they noticed or commented on these or other such things they enjoyed.

If someone you love has been given a gloomy prognosis for their future, it is of course distressing and upsetting. It is only natural to be fearful of the future and to wonder how you will continue to go on living without that person.

You know a grandparent will die and that this is something you will have to experience, but at the same time you hope it will not be for a very long time and that you have a chance to spend as much time with them as possible, learning all they have to teach and tell you.

It is still upsetting when they die, as you will miss them and everything they contribute to your life.

If your loved one has a terminal illness, then on some level, in the back of your mind, you know that their death is an inevitable event. However, that does not make it any easier, in my opinion., as you never can know what the circumstances will be, when it will be, how much you will feel was unsaid or undone, how satisfied you can be, or if you had the chance to resolve feelings or discussions.

If you have had a chance to prepare yourself, then you have the chance to 'tick some of these boxes'.

If you are not there with somebody when they die or have the opportunity to see them in the lead up to the death, you can be left with a sense of panic as you have had no chance to say goodbye. You might feel cheated and that there are unresolved issues. Some families can go through ups and downs and have periods where some members are 'not talking' to others. You should think about whether you want to bridge such gaps and heal rifts while people are still around.

I believe in positivity – staying positive and optimistic – and I feel it helped my family and I to stay positive during Dad's illness. This did result in me feeling somewhat conflicted as I knew in my heart that he would not survive. His leukaemia had struck so strongly and quickly, but I still did not want to entertain negative thoughts or that reality, so, I tried to maintain hope and stay positive. In quiet moments while alone I would feel upset, as I thought about him not being here and my imagining of the reality of the situation would become overwhelming. I would think about events and situations to come and how they would be different because Dad would not be there.

No matter how positive I tried to stay and how I hoped that everything would work out and go back to 'normal', doubt and fear always raised their ugly heads, and I found myself indulging in some very dark thoughts and questions. I think this is normal and would defy anyone not to encounter these thoughts, even if only fleetingly. I tried not to go on the Internet or listen to stories of how other people with a similar condition made a full or indeed miraculous recovery, as I did not want to get my hopes up. I feel it is important to stay present with the situations you have and the advice being given, as everyone is different and therefore their illness, treatment and prognosis will be different.

It is important to be honest with yourself about what you are feeling. It is fine to admit to being nervous and scared. Of course you are.

'Anticipatory grief' is a medically recognised feeling, relating to the Kubler-Ross model of five stages of grief that a patient or someone close to them goes through – fear, anger, bargaining, depression and acceptance.

I tried to make the most of Dad being in hospital, not only to help and distract him, but to feel like I was doing something useful and to distract myself. In trying to help Dad stay positive in hospital I took in lots of familiar things that would make him smile, and so he could think of all the people who loved him and all the great things we did together. I made a collage of photographs of family members, holidays and his hot air balloons (which was his passion and a family hobby). I also wrote him a letter telling him how much I loved him and how much I needed him to try with all his will to fight and not let the cancer beat him.

As much as I wanted Dad to survive and hoped with all my heart that the treatment would be successful and that he would manage to beat it, as I said earlier, I knew he was probably not going to win, the leukaemia was too fierce and virulent. I began to think about and make notes of what I wanted to say at his funeral.

Many people spend time thinking about when it will happen. How much time might there be for life experiences? Will the person make any sort of recovery? How able might they continue to be? Will there be a chance for some last adventures? How will people react at the end?

There will be thoughts about the future. How much would the person be missed by those left behind and how would they feel afterwards? How would their day-to-day lives continue without their loved one being around?

All very morbid thoughts, but as strange as these thoughts and feelings are, I know they are not unusual. You will feel like you are betraying them, by 'indulging' in mentally mapping out what life will look like and what decisions will need to be made while you also feel that you should be focusing on the here and now and not thinking about life without them. Maybe it's a form of mental self-preservation; that your brain and emotions know that you will have to survive and carry on in the future, so suggest ways that you might go about doing that and that you need to think about this. In doing so, it also reminds you of the pain that you will suffer on the way, though.

I think if anyone else has had thoughts like this, they also come with the hope that the person who is dying does not suffer and that the thoughts are fleeting. Although everyone knows nobody can live forever, this is not something that we discuss. Maybe it would be healthier for people involved to have an open dialogue about how they feel – I believe this is something actively encouraged by Macmillan Cancer Support. If you feel that the topic of their ending was not discussed, your mutual fears, their hopes for you and anything that needs to be said, it can leave another layer of guilt after they have died.

Perhaps people avoid such topics through not wanting to 'tempt fate', or that the conversation would be premature, uncomfortable or not helpful, as it is painful to think about them not being here. But if you do have a chance to discuss the future, you can be left with no doubts, no regrets and less frustration.

When someone has been ill, deteriorating or becoming more frail for a long period of time, it may be helpful to cast your mind back and try to remember them as they were. Try to recall them as they were, as their natural and true self, before the illness or frailty really started; this is the person that they really are, this is the person that you really knew. Try to think of them this way.

Be kind to yourself as you cannot help the way you feel. You will probably appreciate on a whole new level exactly what they mean to you when you realise you can no longer physically share and enjoy a bond, a space with them, anymore.

You will not stop loving them just because they are not here physically, you will just stop sharing your life with them as you had done before.

When you know that they are dying and you are thinking about them no longer being there, it can leave a feeling of panic, which I do not think is surprising. Thoughts such as, 'They are my support, my advisor, who will do this role now? How will I do it for myself? Can I do it by myself? Who will help and support me?'

'This person is irreplaceable – how will I cope?' These thoughts leave a feeling of being exposed and vulnerable.

You will want to remember them. I would suggest there are many things you can do to make the last few months of their life as memorable as possible. Many people will be familiar with the concept of a Bucket List, where a list is made of all the things the person wanted to do, but had not done, with the idea of doing all or as many as possible before you die. Go right ahead!!!

But of course that is not always practical, either from the point of view of health, or indeed financial health. There are many other ways to make memories for the person who is ill or the people they will leave behind. You can go on holidays or outings, watch favourite films together, sort through photographs or even attempt to chronicle the (no doubt complicated) family history. You could even hire a professional photographer to take up to date pictures – even if the person does not particularly want to be remembered that way, it is quality time to spend together and reflect upon shared experiences.

Another idea is to think of a list of questions you might always have wanted to ask them about their life, family, experiences, favourite things and memories.

It may be hard for them to talk about but easier for them to write it down. This can also give you a record of their life as told by them – you may discover things you were unaware of or recollections of events that are different from those of other relatives or your own. Plus, it is in their own handwriting. It may sound silly but it can be the little personal things, such as their handwriting, that can be so painful they can almost take your breath away.

As a free bonus for tips and suggestions for making a memory box and other keepsake items, please visit www.cuddleamemorybook.com

If you do not have the time or opportunity to do any of these things before the person dies, I would suggest in the first few weeks afterwards that you keep a notebook close at hand at all times, to write things down as you remember about them. These can be very important in the future to aid your recollections and can include emotions such as how you felt when they cuddled you or things they did that annoyed or frustrated you; after all, it was a part of who they were, and nobody's perfect. Try to think of their favourite joke or jokes, sayings they had or turns of phrase, and advice they gave you (whether or not you ignored it). You should hang on to and keep safe any notes they wrote to you and photos, including the random and silly ones.

It may seem somewhat unnatural, even artificial, but I'm sure these efforts to make memories will provide comfort and reassurance at a later point.

It may be that when the person realised they were dying, even if it had not been acknowledged, that they began to make preparations for after their death. It is a strange thing to find, that they had thought about leaving and took steps to help you, such as leaving a letter or a video of last messages and advice.

As far as my family goes, I think if we had all had more time together then we would have actively spent more time doing the things we enjoyed, as a family. When someone dies, the memories are all we have and therefore become cherished and almost sacred. I would have loved to have had the time and opportunity to have certain conversations or discussions, watched our favourite films or gone on walks at places we enjoyed.

It may seem a bit forced or a little sad or morbid to create situations with someone before they die, but afterwards such memories of more recent events are likely to form a large part of what you have to remember them by. If the chance was not there to create or engineer them while the person was still around, then once they are gone you might have to rack your brain and think very hard to find something similar.

If you are or have been caring for your loved one while they were dying, then often during this process you will have focused on them and their care and put yourself second. After they have gone, you will no doubt replay events and wonder whether you did the right thing, or whether there was anymore you could have done to delay or prevent this horrible event. These are all natural thoughts and feelings.

If you are currently caring for someone, then trust your judgement and push for the medical help that you think is needed to make their health and both of your lives as easy and comfortable as possible. It is hard to consider your current wellbeing while pre-occupied by someone else's care, but it is important to sometimes take a step back, take stock and get a handle on the situation.

After my dad died, I would take time to sit quietly, make a few notes and revisit all the memories of him that I could; I would, in a sense, 'bank' them and mentally lock them down, as I did not want to forget anything, as those memories were now all we had.

Also, because his death came so soon after his diagnosis, I did not really have a chance to think about it at the time so would look to remember every little detail about life from the diagnosis onwards, so I did not lose or miss anything.

I would also try to remember things from the past; for example, I made a conscious effort to attempt to recall where we went on holiday in a particular year.

The bottom line is that people are precious, they don't live forever and we don't know when or how we are going to die, we can try to prepare ourselves, but I don't think we can ever fully do so. We should cherish and treasure every moment we spend with someone because we can have no way of knowing when they might suddenly not be there any more.

Interesting thoughts

'The love we give away is the only love we keep.' – Elbert Hubbard, (philosopher and writer)

'You never know how strong you are until being strong is your only choice.' – Bob Marley, (musician)

'Grief is the price we pay for love' – Queen Elizabeth II

'Grief is the last act of love we have to give to those we loved. Where there is deep grief, there was great love.' – Author unknown

'The death of a loved one is an amputation.' – CS Lewis, author

Poem of Life

Life is but a stopping place,
A pause in what's to be,
A resting place along the road,
To sweet eternity.
We all have different journeys,
Different paths along the way,
We all were meant to learn some things,
But never meant to stay…
Our destination is a place,
Far greater than we know.
For some the journey's quicker,
For some the journey's slow.
And when the journey finally ends,
We'll claim a great reward,
And find an everlasting peace,
Together with the lord.' – Author unknown

'Never. We never lose our loved ones. They accompany us; they don't disappear from our lives. We are merely in different rooms.' – Paulo Coelho, writer (Aleph)

'I mean, they say you die twice. One time when you stop breathing and a second time, a bit later on, when somebody says your name for the last time.' – Banksy, (artist)

'Unindicated and unknown is the length of life of those subject to death.' – Buddha

'A dancer dies twice. Once, when they stop dancing, and this first death is the most painful.' – Martha Graham, (choreographer)

CHAPTER 2
The Month After

The first month after bereavement is a time of contradictions. Time passes both quickly and slowly; you will feel both nothing and everything, and you will probably feel a heady mix of love, anger, calmness and guilt. You will find your own way to muddle through this surreal time, but you do not have to burden yourself with excessively high expectations of what you can and should be doing. Now is not the time to focus on pleasing other people; you are finding your own way.

'Losing a loved one' is a bizarre phrase because they are not lost, they are dead, meaning their physical form has stopped working. It is difficult to find a phrase that is easy to say or for people to hear, but 'They have died' is the most neutral. Although such an honest phrase can often provoke the most surprise through its bluntness, sometimes it is the easiest to say. As the bearer of the news you are probably still suffering from the shock of the news yourself and will probably hope that, if you repeat the phrase enough, it will make it easier for you to comprehend and accept.

'Passed', 'passed over' or 'passed away' are phrases that people use when talking about the death or a person, which appear to cushion the blow as soft, easy phrases that can help the person delivering the news or the one receiving it. I think 'X has died' is the more honest, but very hard to say or hear for most people, because we do not talk much about death and, when we do, we use words and phrases to make it easier for us. Although saying you have 'lost someone' is not really correct, as it is not them who is lost, it is how you personally feel.

If you know it is coming, you are waiting for the news and I am sure a lot of people think they are prepared – even if it turns out fewer of them actually were. When my dad died, I thought I was ready to cope, that it was inevitable; but as it turned out, I absolutely was not remotely ready for it to happen.

You know in your heart of hearts that in life the people around you will die, and some might die before you might have expected. You recognise that you will probably outlive your parents, but knowing this and at very short notice dealing with the reality of it are very different. Cancer and other terrible diseases seem to touch so many people nowadays that we really should be better at dealing with it. In some cases, you will know a person will die sooner rather than later after such a dreaded diagnosis, and so you have a chance to start cherishing them, talking to them, making memories, taking pictures and to start sorting things out. Is it 'morbid' to do so, or realistic? Every day does not have to be lived in the knowledge that an older or ill person will die soon. Much joy and enjoyment could be had along the way.

Such time for reflection and memory-making is not possible when being told, 'Dad has died', when it is so much more out of the blue. There was no chance to actually say goodbye. If you know to expect this news, then you might have thought about how you will react, respond or feel; but even if it might lessen the initial shock, nothing prepares you for being told that your dad has died.

If you have been told that someone close to you is going to die soon, then you may have a chance to be with them when it

happens, although this may not be something you want to do –
which is fine, it is your decision. – or you might not even get a
choice in it. I was not with my dad, I did feel guilty about not
being with him, but my family were and I am OK with that now, if
not slightly relieved, as I think I would have struggled to forget the
trauma of watching his life disappear. Alternatively, you have the
chance to be at peace with them and the situation, and you could
maybe have familiar items around you to help not only them, but
you too and it might help you to accept what is happening and
therefore be less of a shock afterwards.

Even if you know death is coming and you have a chance to
prepare yourself, I think you are never really prepared, and it will
still be a shock. When someone is dying for weeks or months and
you have to watch them fade away to a mere shell of the person
they were, there is an element of relief that they are gone as they
are now at peace. However, the reality of their passing still hurts.

In this situation, they had not been themselves for so long you
had accepted the 'new them', but death is so final – their body
has stopped working and you can no longer see them, touch them
or talk to them. The memory you are hopefully left with is of the
person before they were ill – that is, the one you had known for the
longest – and you actually might not be as well prepared as you
thought. You had been busy caring for them and organising matters
to make them as comfortable as possible. It can be confusing as
to whether you are mourning the person they were or the changed
person – the 'shell' – near the end.

If you do not know to expect it and your person dies suddenly,
I think the shock is greater; there is so much to process. There is
no easing in gently, over time. If you know it is coming you can
warn those around you what the situation is, but if you have had
no warning, everyone you tell is as unprepared as you were. I have
often thought about people who discover a person who has died,
as I am sure logic takes over and causes you to seek medical help.
People must have to battle such great guilt of wishing things could
have been different.

In my experience, I don't think I shall ever forget where I was when I found out about my dad; like the saying that people remembered where they were when they discovered Princess Diana had died. I'm sure other people will remember the tiniest detail when hearing about the death of a loved one.

Ever since his diagnosis, I had on occasion played out in my head. I wondered how I would react to the news. As it happened, my reaction was everything at once; I think you can go on sensory overload and/or sensory shutdown all at once, I thought everything simultaneously and did not know how to react. It was surreal.

Many of us have watched actresses on films and TV programmes collapse dramatically in shock and floods of tears onto the floor, but my recollection is after recently landing following 40 hours travelling, being told the news while standing in an airport car park, hugging my brothers and my husband. Apparently, I said, 'I don't believe you.'

Just to add to the confusion, because we had cut short our holiday, perhaps part of me was still in holiday mode. The rest of my family had already had some time to process the news, come to terms with it and, while they were upset (really upset), I almost felt like it was up to me to counteract that. I was very matter of fact – 'It is what it is, you cannot change it.'

I went to see Dad at the hospital – I wanted to see him, I almost had to make it real and see for myself. Seeing the body of a loved one when they have died is of course not for everybody, but I wanted to; I felt I owed him a goodbye and that if I didn't I would never really have believed he was gone. I think some people imagine that if they see the dead body of the person they love, that is how they will always remember them, but this is not my experience. If I really try and if I really wanted to, I could remember, but I have chosen consciously not to make that my instant memory of my dad.

Whether you choose to see your person after they have died is completely up to you. For some, they find it gives some closure and comfort, they can recognise that their loved one's life has gone; for others, it is not something that they want or feel the need to do. Personally, I never wanted to visit any of my relatives in the chapel of rest because I was worried that would be how I would remember them. My understanding is that funeral homes or undertakers take great care to ensure your relatives look how you remembered them. Everyone copes with this situation differently. When my paternal grandma died, I saw her so soon afterwards it was like she was still alive, but she looked nothing like she ever had. I remember as she had been poorly and lost a lot of weight, and that is not my instant memory of her when I think of her. I did see my dad, but that was mainly because I had been away for four weeks and I wanted to say goodbye to help me accept that he was gone. In some ways, I wish I had not, as I now have mixed feelings about it. You need to understand that quite soon after someone dies they look like themselves, but they do not feel like themselves – the body is cold and hard and feels so unfamiliar; it is shocking and can tarnish your memory of the person and be almost unbearably, unnecessarily upsetting.

I mentioned earlier in this chapter about the loved one is not lost – though you, the one grieving, might be feeling a bit lost.

It is likely you will have to break the news to someone and it is difficult to find a phrase that is easy to say or for people to hear, but I think 'X has died' is the most direct and honest. Although any other phrase or term can soften the delivery of the news, and honestly, clearly and simply stating the bold truth can be a further blow and increase the shock in the person receiving the news, the simple, direct approach has much to be said for it. As the bearer of the news, you are probably still suffering from shock yourself, and repeating the phrase may even assist in your comprehension of it. Some days, I had to be blunt when telling people almost to aid my understanding and to help me adjust; I'm not sure if a part of me might have wanted to shock people too, as I was still in shock myself.

If it falls to you to break the news to other people, you need to find a way that is comfortable for you and what you feel is befitting of the person who has died. Whether you break the news yourself in person, on the phone, by email or even on social media is entirely your affair. One option would be that in telling one person you could ask them to tell others. You have to do something that is comfortable for you, I think death has a different effect on everybody. Most of the time people do not know what to say, so I suggest you prepare yourself for a lot of phone calls, letters and cards. Try not to feel pressured into communicating with people until you are ready, as it can be very time consuming and tiring to repeat the same story to everyone. Brace yourself for people to not know what to say or to say things which may appear odd or strange, as people behave in unpredictable ways when confronted with news and events that are this shocking in nature.

Personally, I find now that I am just honest and say what I feel; of course, I recognise this is not easy for everybody. I understand how difficult and painful it is to be in that situation and, as uncomfortable as it can be, I generally found that people really appreciate you telling them personally.

Finding out a huge part of your life has physically gone can only be described as a very strange feeling for the first few days I felt ok, not too bad, but I now realise that must have been shock. You may of course not feel anything like this, but I mention it as we all deal with grief in different ways – those who have suffered the same loss you have, may be feeling very differently.

At the time I was of course upset, but not inconsolable; Dad was a very matter-of-fact person who believed that we had to deal with the facts of a matter, life goes on and what do we do next? How can I make sure everyone is ok? How do we arrange a funeral?

My main reaction was concern for how everyone else was feeling, wanted my family around me and became very protective of them. I did not really want to talk to other people because they did not seem to understand how I was reacting. I think some people thought I would be a sobbing mess who could not do anything and were surprised when that was not the case.

Straight after Dad's death, I would be doing something normal like hanging out the washing or doing the food shopping and thinking 'how am I acting normally? How am I doing normal things when my heart and body hurt like they are breaking, but I appear to be fine?' The week after, I remember walking down the street and everyone around me was living their lives, going about their business as they always had, and I just wanted to scream, 'Don't you know, don't you know that the world is the worst place, don't you know how much pain I am in, don't you know how horrible everything is? How much harder life will be now?'

I wanted to jump up and down, shake my arms and legs, grab a person and shake them (!) from pure frustration and disbelief that he was gone – and that somehow I was still functioning.

I felt I wanted the world to slow down, to a pace I could manage – actually what I really wanted was for the world to stop because it kept moving around me and its actions left me reeling. As much as I craved normality, which was actually what was happening all around me, I felt totally out of control at the same time.

My thoughts and emotions were changing so fast I could not process them, I felt like I wanted everything else to slow down, so I could catch one thing and deal with it.

There are some days when it seems impossible to take a deep enough breath in, and that you will never be able to fully exhale, as the pressure on your chest feels too heavy.

At the time, I said I was fine and was coping, but looking back

I had migraines, neck and back ache, and I felt tired. So, clearly there were signs of stress and unhappiness and I was not doing very well at all.

I felt bewildered that I could not seem to keep up with my life, thoughts and myself, everything just seemed to look and feel so different, and I could not adjust, but at the same time, I carried on. It was like there was a 'me' on the surface that everyone could see, who acted and looked fine but under the surface was dragging along a shadow of myself that was weighed down with baggage that I could not shift to make the journey easier.

There were days when I felt I could not catch my breath because there were so many changes and things to process, adjust to and accept. As I said earlier, I wanted the world to stop so I could gather my thoughts and catch up.

I found myself having circular thought trains when performing the most mundane of tasks. I was asking myself questions like, 'Am I doing this right?' and 'Should I be doing it differently?'

While we were planning the funeral, the family had a lot of discussions. When people asked where the wake was going to be or what the plans for the wake were, I made a point of saying: 'It is not a wake, it is a party.' We did not want silence and people sitting around awkwardly, which was my previous experience of funerals, we wanted it to be a happy event, a celebration of my dad's life. There were lots of strange; surprising decisions to make and questions asked that I never thought I would have to answer. One question, and a big one, was over the dress code, and the family decided that, although it is of course respectful to wear black, we did not want people to do so. From previous discussions, it was clear my dad disliked the concept of wearing black to a funeral, so to do so at his would have seemed wrong. We invited everyone to wear colourful clothes to make it feel like more of a celebration, and as a family we deliberately chose bright colours because that is what felt right to us. Even if you can see our reasoning, it might not be what you want to do; and of course it is your own decision to do as you wish.

While preparing for the funeral, one of the things I enjoyed – apart from spending a lot of time with my family, which was a great comfort – was sorting through old photographs of my dad when he was little and then growing up; and trawling through all the old family photo albums of holidays and days out (photography is a family hobby), and then sitting talking about those trips and our memories, and being surprised at how different our memories of certain events were.

We ended up laughing about it all; I think this proved to be therapeutic for all of us. We decided at the funeral to have a couple of large collages of photos of my dad riding motorcycles, flying a hot-air balloon or just laughing. It was lovely, and lots of people enjoyed seeing other views of my dad, to find out about his accomplishments, things he had done that they might not have been aware of, that were different from the person they knew. Some people even go to the extent of organising a video or a slideshow so that people can watch them during the party. There are lots of different things you can do at a funeral to personalise it to reflect who that person is, their hobbies and relationships.

Is there such a thing as a good funeral? They are always a strange, upsetting and downright weird event; but when they are for someone close to you, they are just horrible.

My family said that when we woke up on the day, we expected to feel, to some extent, a sense of foreboding, anxiety or heartbreak, as though we were on an emotional rollercoaster.

I had been feeling so overwhelmed with emotions after my dad died that on the day of his funeral they somehow plateaued to a sense of calm.

Since then, I now find that funerals are completely different, I had previously been to the funerals of my grandparents and family friends, but since my dad died, any other funeral takes me right back to that day and the feelings and thoughts I had. It makes me relive the whole event again.

Some funerals are more bittersweet because people naturally get old and maybe they have been ill and lost their quality of life, so there is an element of comfort, knowing they have been released from that suffering, that their pain is over. But it is of course still painful, you miss them and have to accept the reality of never being able to talk to them, hear their voice, smell their distinctive smell or watch their unique mannerisms. It can be painful and heart-breaking.

The funeral of someone taken too young, too early and too damned quickly is a truly gut-wrenching, physical pain that is almost indescribable, coming as it does with a huge sense of injustice. I can only relate to the funeral of my dad, but I can only imagine that if it were your spouse or a child it would be similar or even worse. Once he was diagnosed with leukaemia, I think I had accepted that my dad would not reach a very old age, so, on some level I expected this event to happen at some point, but not as soon as it did.

On the day of the funeral, I had a sense of panic, should I have gone to see him (his body in the funeral home) for one last time? For some people, this visit will bring comfort, perhaps that they saw the person one last time, and a degree of acceptance; for some, it will be almost unbearably painful. Whether you chose to do that is a personal choice, but you need to be prepared that although they have been made to look like themselves while they were alive, they just do not – there is something massive missing – their life force or whatever it was that made that person who they were.

It is probably best to go with someone else, even if you think you probably will not need them, and even if they do not come in with you – you just do not know how you will feel or react, or what you will want to do afterwards – talk or not talk, go home or go for a coffee. Or something stronger.

As we drove to the funeral, I felt like my insides were made of ice; I felt literally freezing, my hands were shaking and it was as though I was in a trance, my body going through the motions. I travelled with my mum and brothers, and we even cracked a few jokes. It is an almost surreal experience.

This is life going on. Someone dies, there is a funeral.

The bittersweet part is that although it is an inevitable event after a death and you will probably go to a few throughout your life, the ones of those closest to you are the hardest. It is such a conflicting event because of the horrible physical pain, but then there is the opportunity to have family and friends all together afterwards to socialise with, to swap stories with – some of which you knew, some you did not; some you had thought were just legends, some you might have forgotten.

Looking at and sharing photos and seeing that person with other people they loved in places they loved, you cannot help but think they would have loved this and it is in some respects enjoyable.

I have often found when I am going to a funeral that my second thought – after the seriousness, the reality of the event that is looming – is to the weather. If it is sunny, I think, 'Great, it's a lovely day for a funeral – an event.' But that seems almost wrong, as though it does not fit. And if it is raining or overcast, somehow this is more appropriate as the weather is more sombre and better suits the mood. I wonder why we think we have to be sombre, downbeat and almost miserable at a funeral, as though to be otherwise would be inappropriate and disrespectful to the deceased. Would they want people to be upset and miserable?

The people who go to a funeral are all there because they had a relationship with that person, your loved one, they are all suffering too; of course, to a different extent, but they still feel the loss.

How different cultures approach and deal with death and funerals will be addressed in a later chapter.

No one will fully understand the extent of your pain and misery as they are involved in their own lives, and if they are able to they will be sympathetic. If they have been through something similar, they will be empathetic.

I felt like the only people who understood what I felt were my mum and brothers, but even then our reactions and coping methods were all very different. Never feel bad for how you feel. One of the hardest aspects is that everyone will want to know how you feel and want to support you, but it's hard to let them do so. Grief can feel like such an isolating experience.

The day of the funeral was one of the most conflicting days I have ever had in my life; on the one hand, I was looking forward to 'getting it over and done with', but on the other, I did not want it to happen, because it felt like the end and that dad had really gone. I had wanted to write a eulogy for my dad, as I felt I wanted to give him the send-off he deserved, to be the last thing I could do for him. I wanted everybody to know the reasons why we loved him, why he was so important to us and the gap he was going to leave in our lives.

I had made notes for the eulogy but had actually only got around to writing it on the day of the funeral. I got up very early while everybody else was asleep, and the words just flowed out of me. On the morning of the funeral, time seemed to just fly by, and the moment was approaching fast, but it also seemed as though it was dragging. I felt a sense of calm overriding everything; I had to, in order to counteract the flip-flopping emotions that were just too much.

I felt like I could not get too upset and emotional because I was worried that if I started crying then I was not sure how I would stop. When we arrived at the crematorium, I knew everybody we had invited, but I had not expected it to look like so many people – there was just a sea of faces everywhere. I had asked my brothers to come to stand with me when I delivered the eulogy, as I had written it on behalf of the three of us. When we stood up and I started to say the words, I could feel a lump in my throat and my voice began to waver. One of my brothers rested his hand on my shoulder to calm me, and I regained my composure and said those most heartfelt words.

Afterwards, I did feel proud of myself, but I did it more to show the love for my dad, as the last act of love for him. After the funeral, we were at a venue that was very familiar to us and somewhere we knew dad had enjoyed being. People asked where the wake was; I did not want to call it that but did not want to appear weird calling it a party.

Knowing that I would not be able to speak to everybody, as there were so many people coming, I had prepared some paper and pens and walked round each of the tables and asked guests to write down for me their favourite memory of Dad. I would then later collate them into a collection of stories and memories for us to keep. It was so lovely to hear everybody laughing, talking and telling stories, catching up with old friends and relatives they had not seen for a while. Everybody was having a nice time which could seem weird or wrong, but somehow it was the opposite, it seemed perfect to hear people talking and to hear life going on. I think that is one of the most pleasant things, perhaps the only pleasant thing, about a funeral.

If the deceased has planned their own funeral before they die, it can be easier for the family and any inter-family decisions, as they can be less stressful. It can, I'm sure, be of some comfort to know that the funeral will be just as the deceased wanted it to be and their own reflection of their life. It is worth bearing in mind that friction may arise with a family member wishing to do something more; for instance, to add a personal tribute. At times of high emotion, it is easy to see how someone may feel cheated if they cannot do so.

I did not allow myself to submit to feelings of 'it is not fair' and that no one should ever have to feel the pain of losing someone they love whether it is their time or not, as I thought it negative and unhealthy. However, I could not help indulging in 'if only'; but not 'if only I had done this it would be different and he would still be here', but 'if only I had done things differently I would feel differently now'. Maybe if we had cancelled our holiday to Australia, or I had spent more time with him after his initial diagnosis. Maybe if I had the time off I would have accepted or coped better, rather than 'putting it aside', as I did, to deal with later. Or if we had had more honest and frank conversations, then I would not feel like I had left things unspoken.

I found that in the first few weeks, the shock of losing my dad particularly made me feel very jittery and panicky. I felt as though I had to keep everything and everyone that was important to me close, in case I lost something or someone. I had to keep it all held tightly because I didn't know what I was going to need in the future; for example, memories of my dad and objects of his. If you are supporting somebody who is going through a bereavement and they are behaving erratically, it might be because they are panicking, clutching at straws and trying to keep everything close, whether that is the emotions, photos, belongings or anything associated with that person. I became very anxious about losing other members of my family, about not wanting to miss anything, and I became very aware of time passing; because, as time went on, went forwards, Dad's presence had stopped and seemed that little bit further behind. It felt hard leaving him behind, which gave me a sense of panic that I did not want to forget anything. The panic I felt was similar to the feeling when you leave the house – you have a sense that you have forgotten something but cannot for the life of you remember what it is; or of being late for something important – you know you should be there, but you get a sick feeling in your stomach and struggle to breathe through the anxiety because you are not there. It is like trying to run really fast in a dream and not getting anywhere, your adrenaline is pumping to make you move and you want to move fast, but there are other aspects keeping you still.

It feels as if time is moving on without you or past you, and you keep being swept along and you just wanted to stop time – so you can catch your breath and get a hold of what is going on and remember them – how they looked, smiled and laughed – so they do not feel quite so far away. This sense of panic is indescribable, and even now when I think about it the panic from that time can make my heart race. It is like being on a bungee rope and trying to get something but being pulled back when you are close – so close – and despite how hard you try you just can not reach it, this is a tiring process.

The memories feel like they will fade or are fading already, and soon you will not be able to remember them. Again, this can cause a sense of panic, which is why I started to write my memories down as they came to me.

There is a sense of shock when you lose somebody, whether you know it is coming or not because nothing prepares you for the feelings and reactions that you have at this time, and grief is as personal as a fingerprint.

You will never know how you will respond, feel and act at that time when you are told the person you love is no longer living. It is similar to a car accident in that you cannot quite remember the impact, but you can see that it has happened; it seems unreal yet never more real.

It is perfectly normal and well-documented that people who have lost somebody struggle to sleep properly. You feel lonely and overwhelmed; your brain has a lot to process, and with a whirl of emotions and thoughts going on you can feel very distracted. I stayed at my mum's house for a while afterwards, and we spent a lot of time together, talking in the middle of the night and crying together. As the weeks went, on I couldn't sleep. There was a part of me that did not want to go to bed or to sleep because I did not want it to be tomorrow as that would mean, as I said earlier, that I was one day further away from my dad. It had begun to seem like a long time ago because you start off by saying 'yesterday', which becomes 'a few days ago' and then 'last week', then 'a few weeks ago' and then a month ago. I felt panicked and resentful of this passing time. I felt very overwhelmed with emotion but could not cry about him. I could not sit in a chair and think about him and cry, but if I were watching the TV or a film, or listening to music, the slightest thing would act as an emotional trigger for me. This became the outlet for my own personal grief.

People deal with the not sleeping in different ways whether that is using sleeping aids, including medication prescribed by the doctor or herbal remedies. A massage can help too or for a few people I know, they tried just generally keeping busy to the point of passing out with exhaustion.

If you do manage to sleep during this time, it appears that it is quite common to either not sleep very well or to wake up very tired after a night full of intense dreams and random thoughts. I am sure if you manage to sleep, there will be a few moments when you wake when you can forget what has happened – and then it hits you like a moving bus, and you have a wave of the same shock and grief, as though it were new.

I have had people tell me that, after they had lost somebody, they have dreams about them; they have conversations with them or relive memories during the sleep, which they found very comforting.

It is of course perfectly understandable if you spend the first few days or weeks feeling numb, with almost a sense of disbelief. You know that they are gone because you have to organise a funeral, and tell people that the person is not here anymore. People will be sending cards, there will be lots of phone calls asking you how you are, and while the rational side of your brain will be able to deal with all of this because you have to do so, and you will want to give your person the send- off that they deserve, the more emotional side of you might well be in total disbelief that you even have to do these things.

I tried to stay positive and think, 'Well, at least they are not struggling and suffering anymore', and in one sense was comforted by this, I knew the pain my dad had gone through, and you are of course aware that life is not permanent.

I guess you can reason this rationally, but having to deal with the reality that somebody is no longer here is really difficult. The logical side might say, 'everybody dies', which of course is true; but people do not always think about the implications and ramifications for everybody else who is left behind.

I went through a difficult and near-constant internal battle, trying to be positive with the knowledge that Dad was no longer suffering and that everybody dies in the end. But what I also felt was the raw emotion, emptiness and pain, and cold, hard reality of the fact that I was never going to see or talk to him or my grandparents again.

In the first few days, you might feel a bit like a zombie, going through the motions of getting up and dressed – maybe eating, going out; possibly going to work; hopefully sleeping; but living your life on autopilot, feeling like you are running on empty, while the stress and shock you are feeling is somehow transformed by the body into lots of adrenaline to keep you going. This adrenaline is the main thing that will be getting you through, but at some point of course you have to pay it back.

You can easily get to a phase where you are tired, weary and exhausted; where you feel you cannot do anything, and that your brain and your heart will hurt so badly that your mind has to shut everything down.

People will suggest that you stay positive, and however hollow they might sound, there is comfort to be had from sayings such as, 'Well at least I had my dad for 33 years of my life, he saw me get married.' But ultimately, what you are dealing with is the reality that there will now be a big full stop in your life, and after that point your life is different. You are of course trying to adjust and accept that life has changed. It is akin to reading a sentence in a book, and halfway through the font changes – it is the same but different; it is your life but it has changed, undergone some fundamental punctuation.

> Go easy on yourself, you cannot control or
> help the way you feel.

We have all heard the phrase broken-hearted, and while I think we have probably all suffered a bit of teenage heartbreak, until you have had an experience such as losing a loved one (in my case, my dad), you cannot comprehend the depth of physical reaction and visceral nature of the actual physical pain. There were days when the aching pain in my heart – caused by the knowledge that I would never speak to Dad again, would never hear his voice, would never have a 'dad hug', could never ask his advice – was so immense and so overwhelming, it really was as though my heart was broken.

It is the sort of pain that knocks the breath out of your chest, makes you want to throw up, makes the blood run cold and head pound to such an extent, I would need to sit down and close my eyes. It could leave an ache or pain in my chest that would last for hours. Sometimes, this could come out of absolutely nowhere, or it would worsen over a period of time. The pain could be brought on by the most random, insignificant thing; I could be quite OK in a given situation, and a seemingly unrelated comment or the sight of something memorable would stimulate a recollection so strong, the pain would instantly become nigh-on unbearable. These incidences will become less frequent – time is a healer, as they say, however, they still happen to me on occasion, even now, six years later, and they can still be strong and completely distracting.

Going back to work is a harsh reality because you just do not feel ready, not that you would ever feel ready; you do not want all the questions, you cannot prepare yourself for how people are going to treat you or respond to you, you may have to explain to customers and colleagues why you have been away and there may be questions that you do not feel ready to answer. For me, the idea of sitting at home and staring at the walls seemed like a waste of time, so I did not want to do that.

Although I thought I would probably need 'quiet time' at some point immediately after the funeral or immediately after the death, I did not feel like I needed or wanted it then. Some people find it too hard to go back to work and end up having a very long period of time off; some people go back to work very quickly because they want the distraction of keeping busy. You have to do what feels right for you.

I think the key is communication. It is great if you are lucky enough to have a good employer who you can talk to and come to an arrangement where you maybe work half days, or if you are feeling you need to go home one day because you really cannot cope that they will be understanding. Inevitably, some colleagues, clients or customers will have different ideas as to what you should be doing. If you are at work, they think you should be at home; if you are at work, then you should be looking for the distraction of work, the normality, that you recognise life must continue; the show must go on.

The nature of my job is that I am client facing and have to shelve my personal life to give my clients my all, plus perhaps unfortunately I had just started a new job when my dad was diagnosed with cancer. As he was ill for such a short period of time, I was still getting to know new clients after he died and, in retrospect, I can see this was a very difficult situation and time for myself, my new colleagues and boss, and my customers. While I thought I was being professional and putting my personal life aside, I think I came across as being cold and difficult to get on with. My approach was very matter of fact – my dad has died and there is nothing I can do to change that; life goes on. That was my dad's philosophy, so, I got back to work, tried to get back to the thing that I could control, that I knew I was good at, and hopefully would find comfort there.

In retrospect, the reality was very different because I was in a new job. I was learning new and challenging things – new, high-tech and high-end techniques and procedures – and meeting new clients who expected a high level of customer service. Because my brain was busy doing lots and lots of things, I was very emotional and not sleeping properly. I had a steep learning curve and was struggling to retain what I was being taught properly, which led to me becoming very anxious and losing my confidence in something that had always given me comfort, and in which I had taken a lot of pride.

It is worth studying your employment contract and seeking advice as to the basic legal minimum your employer is obliged to provide for you. It would also be useful to talk to your employer, outline how you are feeling – doing so is not weak or shameful – and perhaps negotiate time off. There is no shame in being signed off by your doctor from work for a period of time if you are struggling, and your employer would have no grounds to dismiss you or 'force you out'.

If you attempt to soldier on, I don't think it does anybody any good in the long run. If you think you can cope with returning to work then that is fine, we all muddle through in the best we can as it would be a distraction but I would hope employers would not make you do something that in the long run might be damaging to your health, work relationships or, worst case scenario, make a mistake that causes an accident at work through lack of concentration. This can be the reality of grief, that you can easily lose concentration. Maybe think about booking a holiday or some time off for a few months after returning to work; although, if you have lost a partner this can raise its own set of issues, as you are used to always having gone on holiday with the other person and sharing those experiences with them. Maybe you can find a friend to enjoy the holiday with. Alternatively, there are several travel companies nowadays that specialise in breaks for single people.

The first few weeks I spent most of the time not knowing how to feel. I think the closer the relationship the more intense the feelings – the more real it is, and the harder that reality. Some days I could tick along and cope, I would appear happy, at least on the surface; while other days I wanted to hide under the duvet. Some days I wanted to go out into the world and do something massive to make myself feel alive.

At the beginning, I felt I was quite normal, although I was upset, I was confused too, so therefore I found it hard to cry or 'to be upset'. It is only as time passed that I began to feel more despair, hurt and anger, that is when all the other emotions started to become more extreme and then I felt even more confused.

These flip-flopping emotions and the confusion they created were because I felt quite conflicted, because one minute I would feel angry and hurt, and the next I would feel philosophical and reasoned; then I would feel angry again that I was being reasonable because it felt so unfair. The whole experience was just exhausting because your mind is in a constant battle. I felt there was no point in being upset because it would not change anything, then resentful that I was put in a position where I felt I had to be reasonable. I felt helpless and lost, I had lost somebody important to me, and I could not change it.

As I said earlier, there is no right or wrong way to grieve, you just need to ride it out, survive it the best you can. People say time is a great healer, but I do not feel healed by time – I feel less broken as time has passed, because some days it is easier to accept than others. I will still notice that they are not there, especially when I am doing everyday, mundane tasks, and when I have got questions which my dad would have been the best person to answer. I still notice that they are not there, and it still hurts, it is just that I am less likely to end up in floods of tears. I can understand why people stop eating and make themselves ill when they are grieving, as the swinging emotions can make your head spin so much that you feel sick, and of course you lose your appetite.

It is OK if you feel resentful, you probably end up feeling resentful of the fact that the person is not there anymore, resentful that you have to learn to live a new and different life, that you cannot make any more memories together. You might resent that they left you while other people still have their loved ones; feel resentful of the fact that one day you are going to have to accept it; resentful that eventually you will move on and all you really want is to go back to how life was before. You might feel guilty at feeling resentful – or of course even resent it.

There seems to be an expectation of grief and grieving, I think that is because we do not really talk about it so nobody knows how other people have done it so they do not know how to do it themselves or what to expect.

But there is no formula, apart from to be kind to yourself; trust the fact that you love that person, they made your life better and that you will always miss them. I wrote down all the things I could remember about my dad – the good things and bad things, because he was not perfect, no one is, and there were some things he did that really annoyed me or wound me up, but that was part of him and one of the reasons I loved him. I felt it was important not to remember him only with rose-tinted glasses, as I'm sure is quite common for daughters to think about their father.

Be kind and gentle, go easy on yourself, you cannot control or help the way you feel, and cannot will yourself to feel something else.

The feeling of guilt is really difficult because you feel guilty for living as your loved one is not; you feel guilty that you are 'bothering' others; guilty that you if you do go to work you cannot function as well – or if you stayed at home you would feel bad for doing so.

I felt guilty because I had thought about my dad dying while he was alive and I hated that, it was like I had 'thought him away', worried about him not being there, rather than cherishing his presence.

There is no right or wrong way to grieve, but it is important to just be honest about it and to not feel that you need to apologise. I felt like I wanted to apologise a lot – to my friends, as I could not talk to them and they wanted to do so, so I withdrew. I felt bad for crying with people in situations that were 'inappropriate' – at work with either colleagues or clients, as it made people uncomfortable. I felt guilty if I cried with my family in case they were, to their mind, coping, and my crying made them upset.

I might have thought I wanted normality, but the truth was that I had a new normal – a new life and reality, but I could not get a grip on what that was or what it looked like. I felt as though my limbs were dead weights, I was moving so slowly and everyone around me seemed to be doing the same things they were probably always doing, and with an ease and fluidity I could barely imagine.

For me, the week after was actually quite enjoyable, we spent most of it together as a family, laughed a lot, talked a lot and sorted stuff out. We shared memories and saw friends. Looking back, those first few weeks to a month were strange, almost like a 'phoney war', because you can go that long without seeing or speaking to a person when you are away on holiday. They might not have been gone at all.

However, there was some underlying tell-tale behaviour that I was grieving and struggling, such as I never wanted to go to bed at night because I did not want a day to pass, for it to be one more day since I had seen my dad.

I also enjoyed several glasses of wine most nights, which is out of character for me. I can understand how people turn to alcohol in these situations because, much as it can make you more emotional, it can make you numb and help stop you thinking. People want to handle you with kid gloves or like you're made of glass, but because at this stage I felt largely normal and OK, I wanted to have regular conversations and not have to constantly reassure people that I was fine; this really used to frustrate me.

I think when I was talking to other people, I was looking for routine and normality and, for the most part, genuinely felt OK and able to function.

I personally had to do my grieving in private, so when people asked how I was doing I said, 'OK'; partly because I was OK, and partly because I did not feel comfortable telling people, no matter how close I am to them, what I really felt. That would have meant several times a day acknowledging in public that I really missed him, and that I felt that there was a huge part of me missing. I think I was so overwhelmed with whirling emotion, it was difficult to quantify it, to get a solid thought or emotion long enough to articulate it, so therefore, I was OK.

During this first month, we started to tidy my dad's clothes and belongings, and suddenly everything had a memory or sentiment attached that had increased ten-fold overnight. The reasonable and rational parts of me knew it was just things, objects; but the emotional, broken me was not ready to let go, as it felt like part of him was going too, this is the reality but a metaphor at the same time. Because I could not get these two aspects to balance out I felt more helpless and hopeless and, as a result, a failure. I have heard of people leaving this job until months and even years after; and others who just get rid of everything almost overnight.

I think this is your judgement call to do how and when you feel it is right. There are companies that can help and if it gives any reassurance or comfort you can give things to a charity shop, so your loved one's possessions can be repurposed and benefit a charity. If you need to do it in stages, take the things that have the least association first and then, when you feel ready to sort through it again, see if you feel the same way about everything.

Quotes and Poems

They say there is a reason,
They say that time will heal,
But neither time nor reason,

Will change the way I feel,
For no one knows the heart ache,
That lies behind the smiles,
No one knows how many times,
We have broken down and cried
We want to tell you something,
So there is no doubt,
You're so wonderful to think of,
But so hard to be without' – Author unknown

'In this sad world of ours, sorrow comes to all… and it often comes with the bitterest agony. Perfect relief is not possible, except with time. You cannot now believe that you will ever feel better. But this is not true. You are sure to be happy again. To know this, which is certainly true, will make you some less miserable now. I have had experience enough to know what I say.' – Abraham Lincoln

'Grief is not a disorder, a disease or sign of weakness. It is an emotional, physical and spiritual necessity, the price you pay for love. The only cure for grief is to grieve.' – Rabbi Dr Earl A. Grollman

'The very worst part of grief is that you can't control it. The best we can do is try to let ourselves feel it when it comes. And let it go when we can.' – Grey's Anatomy (TV programme)

CHAPTER 3

Three Months and Beyond

Something that played on my mind after about three months was the thought of 'what if' about everything. It is an easy cycle to get into and hard to escape from.

I felt I needed to be stronger, not to indulge in thoughts such as, 'What if I had done x instead of y, would there have been a different outcome?'

One thought I had was, 'What if my dad's leukaemia had been diagnosed earlier – might the doctors have been able to help him?' This way madness lies, there is nothing good that can come from thoughts like these, and they do not achieve anything. I wanted and needed to convert that negativity, that negative energy, and use it to motivate me to use it for good, for something positive. Even if it was just to be motivated to look through some more of Dad's belongings.

I found that if I was having a disagreement or a row with somebody, my feelings would very quickly become more heated and were about more than the dispute at hand, and I would get very upset about my dad, or my granddad.

Looking back now, it's clear to me that I became prone to over-reacting to things. I think this is understandable and would appeal to those closest to you to have patience. If you are not handling matters well, or are feeling overwhelmed, you simply do not have the mental capacity to cope rationally with anything else bad that occurs that needs handling mentally, processing or coping with. A little dispute can therefore quickly become a blazing row, as the dispute is 'the straw that broke the camel's back', and is the one thing that was too much to bear.

You cannot always expect other people to know exactly how you are feeling, even if you are desperately unhappy, frustrated, angry and tearful, and feel it is surely plain for all to see. People are not mind-readers, as much as you might want or need them to be. I kept going, as I did not know how to stop; it felt almost that I had to think what it was I needed to think about – just what was the problem? If I was going to stop and sort myself out, I needed time to work out what I needed to sort out – yet I could not get a grip on what I needed to understand. This just shows the cognitive gymnastics the overstretched and bewildered brain can do at times.

I needed to sort my head out before allowing myself time to process, accept and adjust to the loss. I felt like I was going to explode with frustration as I tried to process everything or get any perspective, my mind would flip-flop from one emotion to another, from one thought to another. I would think if only everything could just damned well stop, just so I had time to sort my head out and get everything in a straight line – get my ducks in a row.

I tried to make sense of life and get some sort of order, but I was trying to reason with myself. On the one hand, I knew that Dad was dead and I could not do anything to change that; on the other hand, I was resentful that he had gone and wished it was different.

I am sure it is natural and understandable to feel resentment and for this to spill over into unrelated matters of everyday life. You could find yourself resenting someone else's apparently great life; everything goes so well for some other person, they still have their parents, great relationships and satisfying jobs, while all aspects of your own life pale in comparison and are under strain from your situation.

After my dad died, I felt more vulnerable. I saw myself as part of a tree, and I was now getting nearer the top and feeling more exposed and unsupported. I felt a new sense of being an adult, of taking greater responsibility, being pushed into this role as I had lost a parent.

Grandad died exactly four weeks after dad, and I was relieved for him. His death was not unexpected, as he was so ill and so elderly he could not keep fighting to stay alive. My reaction to his death was that it was less of a shock, so I did not feel the same level of turmoil that I had a few weeks previously. Although I was still upset, I think I was still getting to grips with the reality of the death of his son, my dad, and to some extent Grandad's death was eclipsed, but it also fuelled the grief I felt for my dad, and I actually have very few memories of this time. This illustrates the huge, painful impact the first bereavement had, because after the second, it affected my life, my memory and my ability to cope with what had happened.

I found that as time went on and more distance was gained from the events, people started to forget, or at least seemed to forget, that my dad had died. They stopped asking and went back to treating me like normal. This is what I wanted at the beginning, but as time went on I felt delicate and unpredictable and generally very fragile. I think at the start, I was in a shock and denial phase, so I did not want to or could not talk about it. I did not even want to think about it, but everybody else seemed, at least to me, to be obsessed with talking about it, while I just wanted to forget and not think about it.

Then as time passed and I was starting to process it all, the reality began to kick in, and everybody else seemed to behave like nothing had happened. This felt really disrespectful, because it seemed that they had not just forgotten that my dad was not here anymore and that I might be in pain, but they seemed to have forgotten him altogether. This added another level of anger to my existing feelings of injustice that he had died.

I did not want people asking for the first few months afterwards, but I did when they stopped asking a few months later. People did not realise and were not aware that after a few months, every song, TV programme, book, newspaper, magazine article or conversation would have some sort of trigger or emotional connection to the person I was missing. This reminded me of the still-raw pain.

In a sense, just as the true reality kicked in and became more painful was when people stopped asking about my dad.

People forget that you are still trying to process not only what has happened and how you are feeling, but also that your life has changed and you are adjusting to it. There will be a new routine and physical adjustments, and you will be missing the interaction and conversations. There is the painful process of sorting out their belongings and removing them, as well as reminders of the person from your life.

It can be the strangest thing that can make you the most emotional, such as finding an item of food in the freezer with their handwriting on the label or a bookmark in a book they were still reading. These are the acts of a living person.

These little reminders can be really difficult, and you might feel silly saying in conversation with someone, 'Oh I found this and it's made me really upset.' Because it is difficult for others to understand, and the more that people seem to have forgotten the more painful and frustrating it is.

It is very hard to go back to work and have other people interact with you as before and expect you to function just as you did before, because for me, every task seemed harder, every job seemed bigger and took far longer. People do not seem to understand that you are distracted and pretending not to be, I could not concentrate as I had before; I wish I had set up a safe word or a phrase to be able to give people around me some indication that I was having a difficult hour or day. I wish I could have had the self-awareness and found the courage to say, 'I'm struggling today,' or 'I don't think I can do that to my usual ability because it just feels too difficult,' as that was how I felt.

In this situation, I am sure people would probably have been understanding, as they might not have realised how much I was still struggling. Some days, you might feel able to throw yourself into a task and behave like you did before because you feel confident and ready to return 'to normal'; and there could be other days where you will just want to find a distraction, hide in the corner or lie in bed wrapped in the duvet and forget that the world outside exists.

Not many people will remember that birthdays, Christmas and anniversaries will be really hard, they might for the first of each of those, but they will not appreciate that they will continue to be tough too and are likely to remain so for several years. Those friends and colleagues who do remember the significance of particular dates may possibly not want to mention it anyway to avoid upsetting you. I find it hard and get annoyed when Father's Day approaches as I cannot buy a card; or I feel like I should not buy a card at all. Even within my own family, I am uncertain as to acknowledge certain anniversaries, as I don't want to upset them if they have not remembered. They could be upset at the memory and then even feel guilty for not remembering, as though it was somehow dishonouring my dad.

I think that, as much as you may find it painful, hurtful and disrespectful that people in your inner circle such as friends and work colleagues forget about your bereavement and that you might be struggling, it is hard to expect them to remember – after all, they cannot feel your pain the way you do. That is why I think the code word or phrase is a useful idea for all, because you are less likely to feel resentful; you don't have to be rude or feel awkward, and they do not have to feel guilty or embarrassed that they have upset you.

There is no right or wrong way to grieve, and there is no need to apologise.

At my dad's funeral, a guest had mentioned to my mum that life would probably become tougher at about three months after my dad's death. I am not 100 per cent sure that I understand why, but there is something that happens around this timeframe, and you just lose the plot – I actually thought I was going mad.

The reality seems to hit with a renewed intensity and grows from a snowball to an avalanche in a short space of time.

This seemed more noticeable with the bereavement of my dad, not so much with my grandparents, but I suppose that the impact was greater, the upheaval more complete and the adjustments harder after his death

Three months is a strange period of time – 12 weeks, 84 days, one quarter of a year. It can feel both a long time and no time, but so much can change and has changed. The numbness starts easing and is replaced by feelings, in my case, I felt an aching hole in the chest, to me, it was as though there was a physical hole that you could see through.

If you go on holiday, you can go without seeing or speaking to somebody for a few weeks; it feels all right to do so. All of a sudden, after 10 to 12 weeks, it's not all right; I found I had a burning urgency to call them, to hear their voice. I started slipping up and would forget. I would think, 'Oh, I'll ask my dad,' and then realise that I could not do so. It gets harder to accept and adjust to.

The dull numbness of the initial shock faded and was replaced by an overload of thoughts and feelings, which made me dizzy, and I felt I was going crazy, along with already being very forgetful and struggling to concentrate.

The most extreme example of this madness I have is what

happened to me. One of my husband's best friends offered us the chance to get away for a few days to his family's holiday home in Spain. We had had a lovely, relaxing few days – my husband, our friend and I. It was good to have a break from home and from work.

We had been drinking quite a bit, which I do not recommend really as it I think on reflection it makes everything more exaggerated. After an afternoon nap one day, I simply got up and walked out of the villa and took off down the street, barefoot, wearing just shorts and a bikini top. After a few minutes, my husband caught up with me and asked me where I was going, to which I responded I was going to look for Dad. My husband held my hands, looked me in the eyes, and said, 'He is dead, babe.'

I could not accept it. 'But if I look really hard, I will find him,' I replied, through a flood of tears.

'No, he is dead, he's not here, he can't be found,' he said, maintaining a soft and probably confused voice.

I repeatedly insisted I could find him if I just looked hard enough. My husband was trying to comfort me and later said I kept sort of weakly gesturing towards the end of the road, that was where I thought my dad might be, as we sat on the pavement and I just sobbed and sobbed.

I didn't understand, I just thought it couldn't be true.

I knew logically he was not missing. I knew he was dead and had seen him, his body, but the shock and disbelief hit me really hard at that moment and I could no longer deny that that was the reality. The only thing I could do to cope with the physical reaction to this knowledge was to curl up on the pavement and weep. I don't know how long I was there, probably not that long really, but I have no recollection.

So, although you may not suffer a similar breakdown and find yourself curled up sobbing on a Spanish pavement, while your partner tries to comfort you and probably thinks you've become seriously unhinged, you may experience a harsh, new and surprising realisation of the fact that your loved one has died. I hope your reaction to it is not as extreme as mine was. Six years later and looking back, I now realise how badly I was coping, but I would advise you to brace yourself for such an experience or reality check that feels as intense a physical blow – one that makes you stop and cry. Be gentle with yourself around this time.

Remember, there is no right or wrong way to grieve, and everybody will have a different experience.

Readers may be familiar with the Kübler-Ross model, or the five stages of grief. It is a series of emotional stages first introduced by the Swiss psychiatrist, Elizabeth Kübler-Ross, in 1969, in a book after her work with terminally ill patients. It lists the five stages people go through after a diagnosis of terminal illness; the model has been used in a range of other settings, including those dealing with grief. These stages are Denial, Anger, Bargaining, Depression and Acceptance.

Through my own experience and from talking to other people, I believe these five stages can be experienced all at the same time for varying amounts of time in quick succession; or some days maybe just one or two through the course of the day, or the course of an hour.

Because I found I was feeling all of these things in quick succession, I struggled to pinpoint any one at any particular stage, to be able to articulate what I was feeling to someone else.

In a way, this led me to feel it was easier to process my grief while I was on my own, as I could think and process much quicker than I could speak. This created several issues, first, on some days, my head was spinning and I felt sick from the whirring around in my brain and the flip-flopping of thoughts and emotions. Second, it meant that people around me would get frustrated because I would not, or could not, talk about what I was going through. I also think it is very hard to talk to somebody who does not know what you are going through, because if it is something they have not experienced themselves, they can only imagine they know how you feel or what you are thinking. They can only estimate and must therefore have a limited understanding of the physical pain, whirring mind and sleepless nights.

I found it strange that people appeared to want me to tell them what I was feeling and burst into tears, almost as though they wanted to feel they were comforting me. I did not really want to do that, I actually found it comforting to talk about my memories of my dad, to reminisce about things we had done – probably because these were happy thoughts and were 'fixed'. By contrast, my feelings were constantly changing and evolving. In another quirk of the way we address and talk about grief, it seemed more acceptable to others for me to be upset and in tears than it was to talk about things my dad had done and said; that apparently was 'morbid' to bring up in conversation. I do find that difficult to understand; it also ties in with my suggestion earlier that it is OK to feel what you are feeling, to say whatever you want to say, because your experience of grief will be unique to you, and there is no right or wrong way to grieve.

Sometimes, I did not want to talk about it; sometimes, I just wanted to be in denial of what had happened; and mostly, I just wanted the opportunity to feel normal, as though life was the same. I wanted to gossip with my friends about the same things we had always gossiped about – TV programmes, friends, music, work, etc.

I wanted the chance to not think or talk about what happened and, by not talking and thinking about it, gain some distance from the stress and turmoil of my emotions, thoughts and awareness over my dad's death. With this distance came a degree of calmness, and it is only with time to reflect that I can acknowledge this was the situation at the time.

I felt frustrated and hurt that the people who were trying to help me would not listen to what I wanted, and I wished I had got a better handle on this at the time, so I could have articulated to them why I needed to not talk about it.

The first few months of trying to establish a new routine and learning to live a new way I found extremely difficult. It was also clear to me that my dad would have been one of the main people who would have helped me to adjust and support me in such a situation. There is a gap to fill, which is an emotional reminder of the hole they have left behind. I spent a lot of time contemplating how to put life back together around this time and to figure out what life would look like without Dad. I was not just grieving for the fact that my brothers and I had lost our dad, I was also sad that my mum had lost her soul mate, and that people I had known all my life had lost a very good friend.

I tried to live my life, but I had lost one of my major reference points and, to some extent, I was just going through the motions, everything felt heavy and pointless. I remember once trying to explain to someone that it felt like walking a dog with lead boots on – with an empty lead!

On the surface, everything looked normal, but I could not relate to anything. I could not, or did not want to, express myself because I was not able to clearly identify what I was feeling, so I could not articulate it.

I felt like I was standing on a very fine membrane over a murky depth of unidentifiable matters, thoughts, feelings etc., and I was just about keeping my balance, as with the lightest wind or ripple I was just going to plummet through that membrane and drown in the chaos that was underneath. The emotions of grief were so intense and chaotic that I felt if I just dipped my toe in and attempted to identify and sort matters out, I would get sucked in and not be able to find my way out.

A character in the period television drama, "Call The Midwife," said something interesting to someone who was struggling with grief. She said, 'What peace can you know at this time? You just have to keep living until you feel alive again.'

I identified with this sentiment a lot, the grief and loss you feel may seem dreadful, but it will gradually, eventually, ease a little.

Quotes and poems

'The moral of the story is that grief, to the person of feeling, is a permanent wound, not a transient state.' – Michael Korda, (writer)

'Grief does not change you… it reveals you.' – John Green, (writer)

'May the constant love of caring friends soften your sadness. May cherished memories bring you moments of comfort. May lasting peace surround your grieving heart' – Author unknown

'When someone is going through a storm, your silent presence is more powerful than a million, empty words.' – Thema Davis, (psychologist)

A limb has fallen from the family tree.
I keep hearing a voice that says, 'Grieve not for me
Remember the best times, the laughter, the song.
The good life I lived while I was strong.
Continue my heritage, I'm counting on you.
Keep smiling and surely the sun will shine through.
My mind is at ease, my soul is at rest.
Remembering all, how I truly was blessed.
Continue traditions, no matter how small.
Go on with your life, don't worry about the falls.
I miss you all dearly, so keep up your chin,
Until the day comes we're together again'. – Author unknown

CHAPTER 4

One Year After

After a year has passed, you will find that it does get easier. No longer are whole days spent crying; in fact, you might find you can go weeks without tears or the feeling in your chest that your heart is breaking. The sensation of pain knocking your breath away and the mind like a swamp full of conflicting and whirling thoughts and emotions settle down and eventually starts to feel clearer and less heavy.

Although the rawness of feeling does fade, I still have days and moments when I do feel resentment that Dad is not there. Life will never be the same again, but over time I have learnt to accept that those emotions are a natural part of the process of grieving and everything feels less extreme.

The brutal reality is that the person is missing from your life and they did have a huge impact on you, which is why you loved them, which is why you miss them, and you will always have some pain. Hopefully it will not be as constant and the other feelings such as anger or resentment will subside; you will have more days of acceptance, and before long you will feel brave enough to stick your head out of a sort of 'grief bubble', the all-consuming nature of grief, and realise that actually it has been subsiding – you have been phasing out of it all along. You will remember the view from inside the bubble, and you somehow have learnt to see what else there is in your life around the gaping hole in it, and hopefully you feel a little less broken.

Life will never go 'back to normal' because it has fundamentally changed; you eventually will have to figure out what the 'new normal' is, and will enter a phase of accepting and adjusting.

This may take a while, and you may be accepting and adjusting to this new life now. Maybe you will have stopped cooking for two and recognised there is not another person in the house. But if you actively engage in the thought process of adjusting, you may find you are resenting that you having to do it, to get used to being without the person – but you are on some level already making this adjustment. You can go days, even weeks, without feeling any pain, and then there will be times when you get just as upset as you always did. You will feel as though you are starting again, with the same arguments or feelings that you had at the beginning, such as asking 'Why?' or thinking, 'It is so unfair' or having an overwhelming feeling of injustice at how completely dreadful the situation is. These days become less frequent and the feelings less extreme, and they are easier to settle. For some people, it helps to have a form of emotional crutch, whether that is spending time doing things you always enjoyed together, wearing a favourite jumper or smelling the scent they wore, I'm sure it helps most people to have those familiar items. For me, I enjoy looking at pictures and thinking of all the fun we had or wearing a scarf that my grandma knitted for me, and when I put it on, I still imagine her sitting in her chair watching her favourite television programme while she made it, and the memories and familiarities give me comfort.

You might find you cannot think as clearly or process thought and feeling patterns as coherently as you might have done before, so you can be prone to overreacting or to extreme reactions; if someone upsets you, says or does something hurtful, then it's as though it is the worst problem in the world. Arguments or crossed words can be very problematic. You can become over-sensitive (not that you would want to admit it), and whereas a normal few crossed words could quickly be shrugged off or forgotten, the disagreement somehow becomes a huge argument, perhaps with lots of tears, which quickly become associated with your grief and not so much about the argument. Likewise, any small challenge or hiccup during the day or something that does not go to plan, that would happen on any day and be taken in your stride, becomes a personal attack and insult. Everything feels so personal because you are feeling so broken by the loss of your loved one.

It can seem that everything feels out of control and you can feel useless and helpless, and then probably guilty for over-reacting, while the other person feels guilty because they have upset you; and things can soon become very complicated.

I remember I felt as if I had turned into a stereotypical teenager, where everything would be done with a shrug of the shoulders or a dramatic reaction and a huff, appearing apathetic about everything. You can just feel such despair at life and frustrated that you cannot see or speak to the person that you want to, and these feelings can bubble over into everyday situations.

Do not give yourself a hard time, take things gently, take a step back, try to stay calm, and do not feel bad if you can't get things done as easily as before. Prepare yourself that sometimes you will over-react to problems or bumps in the road – and sometimes rightly so – but sometimes it will be a symptom of the pain that you are feeling. I think sometimes you almost forget that you are grieving, or that because you have had it for a period of time, you have reached an accommodation with it, and it has become a part of your everyday life. So therefore, when you do over-react to things, you can then suddenly realise that you are reacting to the grief and not to the current situation. Over-reacting is an outlet for grief; everything inside your troubled mind and body feels so disconnected and scrambled up that when you are upset about something that feels like it is because of the current situation, but then suddenly memories of the past can be released which can prove upsetting. You can become very distracted by these memories and then lose your focus. I would get so frustrated with my seemingly inability to do the most simple task without feeling like I was making a mess of it, by making a mistake or getting side-tracked by my memories. There were times when I thought I was going mad because I struggled to understand my seeming mental and physical instability and unpredictable reactions to everything. Five seconds after I had reacted to something, I would ask myself why I had just reacted the way I did or over-reacted to it.

Remember, other people you live with or anybody who is in your life on a regular basis will end up tiptoeing around you, because they are trying to be supportive and sympathetic, and also because they do not know when you are going to have an unpredictable moment. This can prove to be frustrating, because you know they are not behaving normally, you appreciate their efforts, but you might find it patronising because you are aware they are not acting normally.

I found that I would return to these conflicting thoughts and emotions; remember, there is no right or wrong way to feel; everything can feel extreme; everything can be confusing; and just getting through the day can be really hard work.

When they are gone, they are gone, and no single, simple thing can mend the hole. The ache and all of the pain has to be acknowledged, grieved and cried over so that you can start to feel less broken. Otherwise, it comes back and emerges in unrelated subjects in unconnected ways, and by working through it is the only way you have to let it out.

I found this very hard to do and would metaphorically turn the tap on just a little at a time, and then quickly shut it back off again if it seemed I was about to lose control if it trickled out unexpectedly, to stop it becoming an overwhelming torrent. I needed an outlet like a film, TV drama or music to help me.

Sometimes, when something had upset me or I'd remembered something that had made me cry, the feelings would all return to such an extent I would feel almost as though I was starting the grieving process again from the beginning.

I dabbled with spirituality, I was thinking about an afterlife and I visited a psychic, as I thought it would help me find reason and give me comfort. This is apparently very common as a way of attempting to find answers or have some last contact.

After a while, I realised it was not the quantity or the frequency of crying but the quality of it. I could not force myself to physically, outwardly cry almost on demand, but I did so every day on the inside. When something was annoying me or I was frustrated, this would often cause emotion to build up. Then it seemed that something small would be the straw that broke the camel's back and would trigger a lot of tears, what was probably a more exaggerated reaction, almost an over-reaction, as this was now an outlet for my grief.

Some days, when I was angry or frustrated or upset from arguing with somebody, I would cry more. I'd even be unsure what I was crying for, whether it was the situation at hand, grieving for my dad or some other reason.

It is not just a case of learning to live with it; it is a case of having to accept it at some point, you will find a way to do so, you must know you have to, even though you do not want to do that either.

It might seem so fundamental or basic that it is as though you are learning to breathe or walk all over again.

I was happy for distractions, to stay active – I wanted to make my life feel like it counted and therefore Dad's life counted; I wanted to continue to make him proud.

Grief needs time, which feels like a luxury, or self-indulgence, but it is not a luxury; it is a necessity. People say, time is a great healer, which is enough of a cliché to make even the strongest person cringe, it is a noncommittal phrase aimed at pacifying, but it does have a grain of truth in it. It is true that grief rarely gets any worse, but it does not necessarily get any less painful with time, it is more that you reach an accommodation with it; you learn to 'be' with it.

For me, 'Time is a great healer' means that you need to take time and be patient; you need to make time to process and accept what has happened. It sounds simple but is anything but.

In a way, it becomes easier to let life be a distraction from grief. Personally, I felt that as much as I did not want to sit and just look at the walls after Dad died, there were several occasions when I needed to stop everything, sit still and give myself time to process – time to think, grieve and remember. I have had to do this a few times to process the next layer of pain and emotion.

Sometimes, getting upset and having a cry can be comforting, as it revisits those emotions after death and somehow makes you feel closer to that person during the grieving process. Even though people would say that it would get easier and, again, that time is a great healer, I remember thinking, 'I don't want to get over it. I don't want this pain to go away. I don't want it to feel "better".'

A counsellor later told me that this could be because these were the last emotions I attached to Dad and, as I had no opportunity to create any new emotions attached to him because he was not here anymore, I clung on to what I did have.

I have since found a degree of peace and, nowadays, I view anniversaries of not just my dad but other loved ones I have lost as a 'remembrance day'. They are on my mind, so I decided that, instead of denying myself, feeling I was being 'weird' or 'morbid', or feeling bad about the day, I spend time doing something I enjoyed with them or something that makes me think of them.

Going for a walk or listening to music that reminds me of them makes me smile and makes them feel closer, it is something I therefore find is comforting.

In the months after dad died, my maternal grandmother had deteriorated so much that she was merely a shell of the person she was, and it had been hard watching her seemingly losing her will to live and just give up. She had always been such a large, commanding personality.

In the days between Christmas and New Year, it seemed we had just about 'survived' Christmas, rather than enjoyed it, with my grandma being ill in hospital. I could also only too clearly remember the previous Christmas when my dad had been home for a few days after his first round of chemotherapy but had been so ill.

Two years ago seemed so far away, when we had all thoroughly enjoyed a fabulous festive holiday; it appeared such a distant and hazy memory.

The prognosis for my grandma was just a matter of a few days and we were waiting for the horrible news that she had passed away and was finally resting and free from the pain of the multiple ailments and problems which must have been dreadful.

It might seem strange in the extreme, but in a way, as I wanted her to find peace, I wanted her to pass away in the same year as my dad and paternal grandfather had too. I feel incredibly guilty and selfish admitting this, but I felt almost hardened to her impending death, resigned to it, and tried to reason that it was inevitable and, after two previous deaths, it was somehow more acceptable. It was almost as though I sought to keep all that misery, heartache and pain into the one box and shelve it ready for all things new on January 1st.

She passed away peacefully on the afternoon of New Year's Eve.

I did not want to start a new year. I felt almost overwhelmed by injustice and panic that I was leaving my loved ones behind

– as I said earlier, having to say they had died 'last year' added a distance to the matter I just did not want.

The feelings I had were so extreme and I felt them physically. I wanted to run or climb out of my own skin and go back in time, and as much as I know this sounds weird, I literally did not know what to do with myself, and this feeling seemed like it was in every fibre of my body.

I was so sad that Grandma had gone, even if I knew she was no longer struggling. I knew that was what she wanted, and I could reason that no one lives forever; but I felt guilty that I was relieved. I mourned her death and thought more about the person who had left us several years before, when she began to be quite ill, not for the person she became, the shell of the person she was, the shell that had stopped working. It is almost like mourning two people.

It was a strange time; my grandma had died and we were again planning a funeral, just as the first anniversary of my dad's death was approaching. I had fresh sadness for my grandma but was dealing with the inevitable surge of grief for my dad. I also had to try to teach my brain not to constantly think 'this time last year' in the build up, as that really made things worse.

I had been told that to grieve one person can take 12 months, but compounding this with subsequent deaths can prolong the process by years. I can really appreciate this it, feels like you don't have time to fully process and adjust before heading into the next disaster. I started to call myself a Weeble – the children's toy which had adverts with the slogan, 'Weebles wobble but they don't fall down.'

Just like a Weeble, I would wobble and almost fall down, yet spring right back and carry on; at least, that is what I though I was doing; or what I was trying to do.

Probably, because this series of events, along with several other big life events, seemed to arrive quite quickly, one after another, with their own set of emotional pummelling to deliver – and which

I greeted with the over-reaction and sensitivity that are common when grieving, – I found life generally very exhausting and was easily overwhelmed. I had feelings that I wanted life to stop – not end, but stop, so I could catch my breath and collect my thoughts.

I regularly felt the need to take a little time out from the day, just to gain a small distance from the realities of my day-to-day life and a little brain space for some perspective. With hindsight, if I had taken time earlier or been a bit more forgiving of myself and less frantic and manic early on, I may not have felt like such a failure at being unable to cope and that life was being lived in extremes of flip-flopping emotions. I say all this only in the hope it could prove useful.

It becomes a vicious cycle; the mind cannot process or accept what has happened or what you are feeling, so becomes anxious and manic; so, you keep busy to not think about it, but you can get overwhelmed or exhausted – so the mind struggles to process or accept what you are feeling, so becomes anxious and manic; you keep busy not to think about it but get overwhelmed and completely exhausted... This of course then exacerbates the seeming inability to cope with anything and slows you down, meaning that you let things such as projects or jobs slide. You need time out and then feel a bit of a failure and guilt at your own, if you like, absence – so throw yourself back into things, go manic and begin the cycle again.

It should be abundantly clear from the above that you need to go easy on yourself, if you end up not entering the above cycle, then great.

The difficulty, psychologically, is that it is not merely about learning to live with loss, but that you do need to accept life will be different and not as you planned or thought it would be. This is something that takes time; you are in a sense grieving for that other life and it will probably take time and energy and prove to be a battle.

This resentment of change, in a sense, can be very strong and is a recognised aspect of the bereavement process, especially when it is not a change you wanted.

The acceptance increases and resentment reduces in proportion, because you realise little by little, without thinking about it, that it is happening.

Accepting that life is not going to be as you had hoped and planned for is horrible. You must live with the change as that is now your reality. They are no longer here, and now you need to review and create new images of what life looks like.

You will surely think about birthdays they will not be there for, occasions such as weddings they will miss and new additions to the family they will never meet; holidays you have planned or that were merely on a wish list will have to be rethought; and the support and presence they might have offered will now have to come from somewhere new. But remember, and never forget, you are stronger than you think – you might surprise yourself just how much stronger.

It is not merely about learning to live with loss,
you need to accept that life will be different.

Adjusting to change is easier when you want it or actively seek it out; however, when it is imposed upon you it is natural to first seek to reject it and only later adjust and accept it. Bear in mind it requires less energy to allow than it does to resist, and that resistance is fuelled by resentment and heartache.

Even if you were able to accept notions of change more readily, or even to talk to your loved one and begin adjusting to this new reality while they were still alive, I feel sure that when it arrived it must surely still have caused shock and resentment – feelings of life is not fair, as you wanted them to be a part of it. They are leaving your life far sooner than you wanted. Hopefully having the chance to discuss with the person while they are still here can assist with this transition to your new reality. Even if it does not and you are still furious, upset, bereft and angry – that is still fine. Your feelings are yours, and all are OK.

I did not want to accept that my dad was gone, and I adjusted slowly to it. It is perhaps ironic as the main person I would have turned to in such a period of upheaval would have been my dad; as he was no longer here to offer me the help, advice and support that he had done before, I had to find it elsewhere. When someone has been a huge part of your life, you know they are there if you need them, even if you do not see them every day or even very often.

To some extent, the process of adjustment and acceptance that has to be achieved is, I think, a bit like learning to breathe or walk again, something that was once so natural is now unnatural, forced and artificial.

During the first year or so, the thing that would frustrate me the most about the impact of the grief was the forgetfulness. On some days, it seemed difficult to function, as simple tasks needed a great deal of thinking about and concentration and became exhausting. I was so preoccupied with memories and pain that I could not retain information or remember what I had done earlier that day. Things were compounded by a lack of understanding from people around me; I struggled at least initially to articulate the problem and, as I didn't say anything, I felt people would get a bit frustrated or impatient with me, leaving me to feel guilty and, particularly at work, would doubt myself and my ability.

I have spoken to many people who have found they became forgetful while grieving, and I am sure it is natural to do so, as you are processing so many thoughts, emotions and adjustments. You have not got the brainpower to do all that and remember more mundane matters such as work tasks.

I found I would get so distressed about this forgetfulness and the repercussions of it that I thought that I had gone mad. I had not seen it starting to happen and could not explain why and how it had – plus, I thought it might be here to stay. It was with relief that

I was seeing a counsellor when it was at its worst. She reassured me that it was a natural part of the process, that it would subside and that I should take it easy on myself and not get worked up, preoccupied or make it worse by getting drawn into a cycle of forgetfulness, frustration, guilt and failure.

I thought I was handling everything OK and keeping 'all my plates spinning' at once, so this forgetfulness was the reality that actually the plates were starting to fall. I was not doing as well as I had thought. It took me a while to see that it had escalated, and by not addressing or accepting there were very powerful emotions that I needed to allow myself to have, that I was in fact making matters worse.

The brain gets so preoccupied with keeping you functioning and having you engage with simple things, that I found it just could not retain all the information and function as it would do ordinarily.

During the first year, I almost manically sought out activities that made me feel alive. I needed a project to focus on so I could push out all the things I did not want to engage with. It felt a bit like moving out of your home while you are having renovations done. The difficult stuff, all the emotions and upheaval, would end up sorted out and level while I was off doing something else but, just like the worst cowboy builders, when I returned expecting a palace everything seemed in a worse state than when I had left.

I was happy for and welcomed the distraction, as matters seemed easier and I felt more positive while doing something else; however, if anything negative happened, my mood would just plummet. It would require so much energy to pull myself back that I became very protective of my positivity and would actively avoid situations that might threaten it.

There is little harm in distraction, but I think you need to be aware that it requires a lot of energy and that eventually these natural feelings of loss and bereavement do catch up with you – you cannot outrun them forever.

It will vary for everyone, and I know some people successfully manage to make a home of this alternative state of distraction and denial, but I feel sure it can only be temporary and the grief cannot be avoided.

From conversations I have had with people, it seems common that a death in the family can lead to breakdowns in relationships, as emotions are high and hard to handle. This is no real surprise, but some fallings-out can be long-term or even permanent. Emotions around death seem to spill over into these extended relationships, whether that is anger, resentment, entitlement, injustice or frustration. To a certain extent, the stresses of grief can highlight strains and cracks in relationships that were maybe ignored or tolerated in the past, even since the death of your loved one.

Then, to these stresses and strains, add in that ugliest of subjects: money.

I think it would be a good idea, in order to prevent long-term damage or permanent breakdown of relationships, to postpone the processing of all wills and estates for a year until everyone's emotions are more settled.

I am sure that potentially volatile situations would be handled better with greater distance from the event i.e. the division of wealth and assets.

It always seems that such items are a replacement for the loved one or act as a proxy for relationships. Some family members seem to feel entitled to objects and money regardless of how it would make others feel, and one hears stories of family rifts over the smallest things – items being taken from the house without discussion and often against the dying wishes of the dead.

Some family members might favour a quick and decisive division of the deceased person's furniture or property, whereas others may suggest a period of more calm reflection.

Everyone has memories of their loved one, and they are often attached to objects, regardless of their worth. Ideally, this is a time for families to come together, but often death, money and emotions seem to mix together to cause untold levels of hostility and resentment. It is almost as though any negativity felt towards a family member before the death can be exaggerated afterwards. People can reveal their true colours.

Personally, I felt guilty spending the money I had inherited, I felt embarrassed that I could buy things I could not before. I treated myself to a nice handbag and did some repairs to our home, neither of which I would have been able to afford beforehand.

Sometimes other people's reactions seemed to be a sort of jealousy that I could spend money and they could not, which made me uncomfortable. I would happily have given back all the money without a second thought in order to spend time with my loved ones again; it is only money and is worthless in comparison.

It seems difficult to explain; I didn't want to be in a position to spend it, it did not feel like my money, and in a way I resented that I had it.

I spent it after a lot of thought and in a way that I knew matched the ethics and mentality of those who had left it, in a way I was sure they would have approved of, which also made me feel close to them. I did things with the money that I would have enjoyed with them.

If you do inherit money or property then it may cause some conflict within yourself. You would rather your loved one was still around, but they wanted you to have whatever it is they have left you. It is for you to do with, spend or use as you wish. The person who left it may have had ideas as to how you might use it, but ultimately it is your inheritance and was left with love. You do not have to justify what you do with it, but others may be jealous or resentful that you have this 'extra' money to spend. They will not realise it is not like winning the lottery and can be celebrated – this money has cost you a lot.

The first anniversary for me was very strange, because a year had passed, but at the same time it felt like both no time at all and an eternity.

When you think about other things that have happened within a year, it is the same amount of time, yet they can feel completely different. Your perception is of a much shorter or much longer timeframe. You cannot help but count off the first anniversary of every special or significant day, and they are really hard. For me, the first event that came up was Father's Day, then Dad's birthday and then a string of family birthdays which were all days I wanted to hibernate from, as these dates would reinforce and restate the fact that he was not here. As the anniversary of his diagnosis loomed, I relived all the days that had led up to it the year before and found I was reliving them very clearly but with a new light. I was thinking about things he had said a year earlier, in the lead up to seeing the doctors; my family and I were discussing occasions when what at the time had seemed a throwaway comment now assumed a new significance.

Birthdays do get easier, but I still feel a tinge of sadness, as there is no card or phone call, however, as time passes you do adjust and get used to it. Eventually, different life events can happen and bring a new aspect to feelings of loss; as people have babies and families grow and change, as people get married, you cannot help but wish they were around to see it and, as such, think about how different the celebration would have been if that person were still there – their absence feels conspicuous.

I actually found the second anniversary to be more difficult than the first, especially Christmas and birthdays, because you prepare yourself the first time round that it is going to be difficult and wrap yourself in emotional bubble wrap to help prepare for pain, but on the second occasion it is easy to think it will be easier and it is not; for me, it felt more raw and exposed.

The first Christmas after my dad's death was really hard because he had been poorly the year before and, even though we tried, it was not a normal Christmas, a time for celebration. And so, thinking of our last traditional Christmas together was faded as it was much longer ago and I had not cherished or 'banked' the memory. I had not realised at the time that it would be the last time we would do certain things – the last time we would all eat a big Christmas dinner and drink a bit too much wine. It seemed I had to go back and remember it anew, and attach new significance to aspects of what was now the last Christmas we would celebrate together.

The first New Year's Eve was so much harder than I ever thought it could be. We had lost three family members in 11 months, and it has always been a mystery to me why the stroke of midnight, the significance of the turn of one minute to another, will 'wipe the slate clean' and signal 'out with the old' and 'in with the new'. It is the start of a new year but it is only the turning of the minute, like any other; in the first few weeks after Dad died, I would often stay up all night, because by going to bed everything was one more day further away. So, the first New Year's Day felt like an absolute bombshell, because by time turning from one minute to another and therefore one year to another, my family members that had died in one year all felt further away. I now had to say they had died last year and, although it was 11 months from when Dad had died, and one day from Grandma, it still felt current and relatively close. The turning of that one minute, it now felt like longer ago and brought a new level of feelings of guilt and inadequacy. When you now must say 'last year', you cannot help but feel that people will expect you to be further on in your grieving process, but it is important to remember that it takes everyone a different length of time to process and adjust – and that is all right.

On anniversaries and birthdays, or days that just seem difficult, distraction is useful and welcome, but there needs to be time to allow those thoughts and sad feelings to emerge, as they are natural, inevitable and part of the process. So, let them come; let them out and remember how the person you are missing would help you celebrate and what they would say to you on that day. Cherish the memories, recognise the pain, and allow yourself to be happy and enjoy what you can.

Father's Day and Mother's Day (depending on which parent you have lost) can also be incredibly hard, and you could feel a bit lost and resentful of other people posting Facebook messages wishing ,'Happy Father's Day', 'to the best dad ever' and asserting 'I would not be the person I am without my dad'. That can really sting, along with seeing the cards in the shops in the days before the event. I'm not saying don't post these messages and pictures to social media, but it's a good idea to let others know you are thinking of them in such a situation and that you understand this day is going to be difficult for them.

I also found the birthdays of the deceased quite tricky and I didn't expect my friends to remember when my grandparents' birthdays were, but my dad's birthday was quite hard, I felt a bit lost, as before I would have been preparing to do something special to celebrate, while not everybody wants to continue to celebrate and acknowledge those birthdays after the person has died.

It seems really hard not to buy birthday and Father's Day cards for my dad, even though he is not here, as it can mean further accepting that he is not here; although I have accepted he is no longer here, he is still my dad and still special to me, so it hurts not to acknowledge him somehow.

As anniversaries approach, they tend to weigh on the mind and can make you feel a bit preoccupied and maybe a little bit emotional that the people around you (unless they are family or very close friends) will not be aware or remember the significance of the date, which can be really hard. You could find yourself in a social situation feeling embarrassed because you are getting upset at what might, to someone else, seem unimportant or even trivial. I think you have to accept that around these anniversaries life becomes a bit tricky and you end up reliving the events building up to those anniversaries and reliving the pain and emotions that you felt as everything feels heightened at such times.

Quotes and poems

When I lost you

I wish I could see you one last time come walking through the door

But I know that is impossible, I will hear your voice no more.

I know you can feel my tears and you don't want me to cry,

Yet my heart is broken because I can't understand why someone so precious had to die.

I pray that God will give me strength and somehow get me through

As I struggle with this heartache that came when I lost you'
– Author unknown

Grief

I had my own notion of grief.
I thought it was the sad time
That followed the death of someone you love
And you had to push through it
To get to the other side.
I am learning that there is no other side.
There is no pushing through anything,
But rather, an absorption
Adjustment and acceptance.
Grief is not something you complete,
But rather endure.

Grief is not a task to finish and move on,
But an element of yourself,
An alteration of your being,
A new way of seeing and
A new definition of self – Gwen Flowers

'You don't get over it, you get through it. You don't get by it, because you can't get around it. It doesn't get better; it just gets different. Everyday… Grief puts on a new face.' – Wendy Feireisen

'The reality is you will grieve forever. You will not "get over" the loss of a loved one; you will learn to live it. You will heal and you will rebuild yourself around the loss you have suffered. You will be whole again but you will never be the same again. Nor should you be the same, nor would you want to.' – Elizabeth Kubler-Ross, (psychiatrist)

'When you are sorrowful look again in your heart, And you shall see that in truth you are weeping for that which has been your delight' .– Kahlil Gibran, (artist, poet and, writer)

CHAPTER 5

Expectations, Hope and Communication

At first glance, it might seem a little strange to combine these three subjects into a single chapter, but I shall attempt to explain how I believe they are linked.

In a sense, other people's expectations around the subject of death, how the family of the deceased should behave and what they should do – and at a particularly difficult and stressful time – create the ideal conditions for a range of misconceptions and misunderstandings.

In the first few months after Dad and Granddad died, I felt very aware of the expectations from others, which made me feel quite defensive.

I really felt the pressure of others' expectations of me and my family's situations. People appeared to have particular expectations of how I would be feeling and what I wanted to do. They thought and that we should avoid talking about dad because 'it might upset me'. It seemed to me that in some cases, people were merely protecting themselves from feeling a bit odd or awkward talking about something that was potentially going to be difficult.

My perceptions were clearly over-sensitive and exaggerated by my emotional state at the time, but other people's expectations added to my own frustrations, as I felt I was disappointing people by not doing what they had thought I should be doing, and then as a result felt guilty for doing so. I felt perhaps I had disappointed them, but also felt they were being a bit judgemental – surely it was acceptable for me to do what I wanted? Were they in a better position to judge somehow?

The dictionary definitions of expectation include:
The act or state of expecting;
The degree of probability that something will occur.
It is also the feeling that what is wanted can be achieved or, realised, or that events will turn out in the best possible way.
Hope is defined by the Oxford English Reference Dictionary as: 'Expectation and desire combined, e.g. for a certain thing to occur.'

I sometimes wonder if hope and expectation get confused; somebody mourning might be told, 'I hope you feel better.' But what they might hear is, 'I expect you to feel better.' There is an inherent burden placed upon the person grieving, that this is how other people expect you to act. They can then feel guilty that there is something they have to live up to – even if this was not what was intended.

When dad was diagnosed with leukaemia, I found that in the first few days I struggled to tell people, and when I did I was quite dismissive of the subject. It seemed to me that people wanted me to tell them every detail, and I didn't know that much, as every patient and treatment is different, depending on them, the type of leukaemia and their treatment. There was so much information coming from the doctors to take in and understand, it was difficult to get across to people. I also felt I didn't want to 'go on and on' about it.

I tried to stay optimistic and positive because I felt any negativity would be harmful and feed upon itself.

I also felt an expectation to feel and portray that a dynamic had changed in our family, that we had to show to other people that we were now a 'family dealing with cancer', but it just felt too strange, too surreal, and I just wanted life to continue as normal – but with added hospital visits.

I felt others' expectations were that dad would get better, as I was repeatedly told about a friend's relative or a neighbour's aunt that had leukaemia and survived – so clearly my dad would be fine. I know this comes from the right place, people want to be positive and optimistic, and to be honest I hoped they were right, but I did not let myself indulge too highly as I wanted to avoid being disappointed.

In the main, I found that people were very supportive and always asked after my dad, about how his treatment was progressing, and I am sure that was also a kind of indirect way of asking how I was doing.

I think people must have no conception as to the degree that you think about the person who is ill; when alone, it was most of the time and to the point of distraction. I was wishing for the best outcome, thinking of anything I could do, but still having to prepare myself for the worst.

So, in conversation with someone else, you might subconsciously be glad of the distraction and the chance to think and talk about something else, but of course they expect you to tell them what is new. In my case, people asked how my dad was doing so they could offer support. It almost seemed that some people expected that I had nothing else to talk about – that there was nothing else that I would want to talk about.

Having said that, it is great being able to talk about what is on your mind, especially when your thoughts are a muddle, and thinking aloud and "venting" helps to make sense of it all.

I found I met with a lot of surprise, along with doubt and

questions when telling others of things I was doing, or planning on doing, while dad was ill, which I think made me a bit defensive.

For example, my husband and I had planned a long holiday to Australia, and we were leaving for a month, just one month after my dad's diagnosis. My dad was clear from the start – he was adamant that we were to take the holiday. It took lots of discussions with several people, sometimes involving the input of my dad and his healthcare team, for us and for other people to accept that he wanted us to go.

When I talked about going, it seemed most friends and colleagues expected that we would cancel, even after I explained it was my dad's wish – that he expected for us to go. Again, I had encountered another one of the unwritten expectations – the social conventions around serious illness and death. I could understand that they were surprised, but it was how ingrained the idea was in their thinking - how could I even contemplate being half the way around the world while my dad had leukaemia? Even if, as you say, he is happy for you to go.

I think I was reticent about going and I had hoped for some support, but other people's expectations gave me the opposite feeling.

I also felt an element of expectation that I was meant to put my life on hold while Dad was ill, without them realising that would have been completely opposed to Dad's philosophy on life.

There was a hope and expectation, as I am sure many others in similar situations have, that he would be cured and that everything would return to a more comfortable place and everyone could carry on as before. No one I knew had gone through the same experience we were now going through, so I had no one to compare notes with or an example to follow. I maintain that we should deal with such upheaval the best we can, in our own way, and other people should learn to be more tolerant and accepting of views which differ from their own.

Personally, I do not respond well to others' expectation of me, it makes me want to do the opposite. After Dad's death, I felt people's expectation of me was that I would want to break down, hibernate, be miserable and cry all the time; that I would want to have time off work and would want a sombre funeral. Some of these things I might have wanted to do - particularly the idea of hibernating – but I just couldn't, I didn't know how.

I felt an expectation that people wanted me to cry, but I couldn't, I wanted to talk about them, because they were on my mind, but couldn't as I felt that people were uncomfortable with this. People would clearly feel awkward and suggest it was perhaps a bit 'morbid' or that I did not dwell on it. This, I feel, is as much to cover for their own embarrassment as much as it was intended to help me.

I also felt Dad's expectation after he died, that life goes on, and I felt I wanted to make him proud and do what he would have wanted and expected, even though I know he would have been worried about me if he had been there.

I don't know whether it was because my dad was perceived as a man of traditions or whether it was a reflection of the belief of others, but some of Dad's wide circle of friends had expected to wear black to the funeral and were uncomfortable (in some cases, visibly taken aback) by the family's request that guests should wear something colourful instead. Again, this may have been my perception, what I felt their expectations were due to how their reactions were read through the prism of over-sensitivity and grief.

It's probably a good idea to expect a mix of responses and reactions from others when you are at the beginning of the bereavement process, as your news, reactions and emotions will make others feel uncomfortable, and therefore they might feel it is difficult to interact with you and could even avoid you altogether.

Emotive events such as a death provoke very strong reactions within people, and they can struggle with their own thoughts, feelings and emotions – and by extension you and yours. I'm sure people have sympathy and are concerned about your feelings, but at some point they must think that your grief and troubles are your own, they are yours to work through and deal with, and they have their own lives to lead.

When Dad died, it was clear people were unsure of what to say to me, even as they felt they wanted to say something, some words that would make me feel better. For much of the time, what people said sounded as though were reading something benign off a greetings card. I am sure they hoped that their words would provide comfort and reduce the pain, but I'm also sure that saying something made them feel better, like they were helping.

I do not think I am alone in feeling anger after my bereavement, I'm sure that must be a common reaction, and maybe I did not want to hear, 'It will get better with time' and 'Well at least he lived a good life', or 'He isn't suffering anymore' because I knew all these things. I was very lucky and grateful to have had him in my life for as long as I did, but I also as a result knew exactly what I was missing by him being gone, and in a way these platitudes made me feel more angry and resentful.

It is hard at this time to separate logic and reason; logically, yes, time will make it better, but you do not want time to pass because the more time passes, the longer it then becomes since you have seen them.

Sometimes, it seems that other people react and respond to things without thinking, and that sometimes I was left so astonished and flabbergasted by the thoughtlessness of what somebody had said. For example, when talking to somebody about how I was going to invest my inheritance money, not only from my dad but also from my grandparents, several people responded along the lines of, 'You are so lucky'. I just wanted to scream at them because I did not feel so lucky, quite the opposite, I would still today give up every penny of the money I had inherited to spend an hour with my dad or grandparents, just to hug them and tell them how much I love them, how hard life seems without them, how much I miss them and ask the questions that I wished I had asked them before they died.

This is another example of miscommunication. I know the sentiment was that it is helpful to have a financial bonus, but they simply do not realise how much you would rather trade it or how a small turn of phrase, intending for you to 'look on the bright side', can actually be really hurtful and offensive.

While we are on the subject of stupid things people say, another one that really aggravated me was when I was getting upset over what appeared to them to be something small or that they did not understand, they would say, 'Do you think your dad would be happy to see you like this?'

The answer I wanted to say was, 'No, of course not. He would never have liked to see me upset, but I also do not think he would expect me to not be upset about the fact he has died.'

Often, this was said by people who did not even know my dad, so it really riled me that they felt they could talk about him or on his behalf.

I was already angry about the situation and that I was getting upset – this is another example of how easily the sense of proportion and perspective can be lost when you are grieving. I am sure what they meant was that they did not like seeing me upset, and maybe if I had read into it better, or they had actually said that, I would not have felt so resentful.

It is OK to feel angry and resentful,
they are typical emotions during this process.

Added to this was the annoyance I felt, as it seemed the person invoking my dad was trying to control my anger, tears and emotions, as the situation was obviously making them uncomfortable – so saying these words would either comfort me or make me realise I was overreacting and stop. So, then I had all these added feelings of guilt and embarrassment on top of the emotions that I was feeling originally.

Exhausting.

I now know a lot of these responses come from people not knowing what to say and feeling uncomfortable in certain situations, such as a person in tears in front of them. But for me, it would have been easier, if they knew me well enough, to just give me a hug. If it was someone I didn't know so well, I wish they had just said something like, 'Take a moment, can I get you a glass of water?'

I am upset. Please just allow me to be so for a minute.

It was not until Dad died that I realised how much people use these benign platitudes, and how insincere and annoying they can be when you are on the receiving end. I am sure there are some people that are comforted by them, but I think they are just trite and too easy to trot out.

Other phrases I heard that I know were meant to be comforting but were not really include:

He lives on in you

Cherish the memories

At least he is not suffering anymore

He is now at peace

Or when I would be doing something fun or positive after such sadness, people would say, 'Time to make new memories or new happy memories.'

These may all be honestly meant, but I felt they offered no reassurance or help for my anger, resentment or sadness. I just wanted to see Dad and my grandparents again.

You may find comfort and peace in such, perhaps traditional, advice, and that you have friends who know exactly how to comfort you. It may be that you can easily express your grief, let out the tears and sadness, and can steadily work through your feelings – in direct contrast to how I did. You might be the sort of person who sits in the middle of both of these extremes.

None of these are right or wrong. There is no correct way, as when you are grieving they are your own relationships to mourn, your adjustments to make and your own ways to cope. As long as you are kind to yourself, you will at some point be able to see that it has become easier, and you may not even be sure when it happened. The length of time will be different for everyone.

In everyday life, people ask how you are, but they do not really expect the truth; no one wants to hear about the various physical ailments you might be suffering, so we say, 'Fine'.

When you are grieving and someone asks you how you are feeling, you know they are only expecting a version of the truth to comfort and reassure them that you are not suicidal!

The truth would probably be too harsh and too much, so we reply, 'Fine,' or 'OK, thanks.'

What you probably really want to say is along the lines of, 'I am depressed and angry and I feel hopeless and helpless. I am out of my mind with tiredness from crying and "feeling". I am trying my best not to think or to feel as it is too difficult, too overwhelming and I don't know how to feel OK again.'

They would surely have regretted asking you in the first place.

I used to actually get a bit annoyed with people and struggled sometimes to keep a straight face and reply merely, 'Fine, thanks.' The annoying thing was that I'm not sure they understood the gravity of what they were asking. When someone would say, 'How are the family?' what I really wanted to say in reply was, 'How do you think we are? Our world has been turned upside down, and I do not know how to think or feel about it. I cannot make sense of it. They cannot make sense of it, and I am trying to look after them, and they are trying to look after me. I do not really think we are helping each other but we are muddling through.'

It is difficult to say this to people so I said I was fine, because to a certain extent it was true, and it was easier; otherwise, I felt I would open a whole can of worms.

Some people will get frustrated, as they cannot relate to your fluctuating feelings and the relentlessness of the pain you are suffering, so they might stop asking how you are. This might be simply because they feel at a loss for how else to help, or that they are not helping because you are clearly still in pain. It is worth considering some outside assistance from a trained professional such as a counsellor.

I know people do want to know, they are genuinely concerned, but I think the question should not be: 'How are you?' but a more helpful: 'Would you like to join me or meet for a coffee and a chat?'

Some people find it hard to talk on the phone, it does seem less personal and they are not there to offer a tissue or a cup of tea. Also, you can gauge how people are managing when you are face-to-face; it is easier to give a hug for comfort or to change the conversation for something more light-hearted. Expect people to communicate in different ways. Interaction from others will vary, but also how you respond will both change and vary depending on how you feel and the nature of your relationship.

I know I did not often give an honest answer because I did not want to think about how I was. I was exhausted by thinking and feeling about how my family and I were.

You also need to be prepared for the fact that some people will not ask you how you are, and you might feel angry and resentful that they have not. This may be, among other reasons, because they do not have the time or energy to listen, or they feel bad because they do not know what to say or do to help, or maybe even that your bereavement has brought up their own feelings they are trying to deal with. I have included this as a warning in case it causes you more upset or makes you more angry and resentful. Grief is a very complex process, and everyone finds his or her own way through it.

Expect miscommunication, misunderstandings and misconceptions, it is only natural when everything and everyone are in a muddle, either dealing with the bereavement or trying to do what is best for you. Try to communicate openly with people about it and don't be too hard on yourself.

Tell them if you do not want to talk about it and need instead to talk about TV programmes; or that you do want to talk but would rather do it over coffee, face-to-face; or tell them that you need a few days first.

Ask them if they are the sort of person that you can ring in the middle of the night when you are awake and upset, or if they are the kind of person you can drop in on without notice. Try not to be too offended or take it personally by people's reactions because for some people your grief can do strange things to their own memories and feelings.

I would expect your feelings and responses to how others interact with you to vary. Some days you will be accepting and some days you will be annoyed, it is an unfortunate reality of the muddle you are left with after bereavement.

Just remember, if you ask an honest question be prepared for an honest answer. Be honest in your actions and you will receive honest reactions.

From people I have spoken to, I know there is a common feeling that after a year others expect that everything is mostly fine and back to normal. They can be surprised when you are still emotional.

I think this is partly because the grieving process is not talked about enough and people are unaware of exactly what might be going on. It could also be that people do not want to risk upsetting you, which is strange. I felt that people wanted me to be upset at the beginning, as if there is a formula to the process that you are expected to abide by.

Expect people (especially those not immediately affected, such as colleagues or some friends) to not remember anniversaries, they may have an idea of what time of year it is but possibly not the date. They are not doing this to be cruel, but it will not make it any less painful. I know I felt silly reminding people why I was upset or struggling so much, as I was almost back to being 'fully operational' again. I find that around anniversaries I reopens old wounds and reignite the pain and the grief. It is not something I can control, the dates are etched in my memory.

When seeking advice from others who have suffered bereavement, do not expect their words to be unquestionably the right answer, and bear in mind that what they can tell you might not be as helpful as you had hoped. Their experience will have been different to your own, just as they are different to you. They will cope with problems and accept support in ways that are particular to them.

They might treat you in the way they wanted to be treated when they were grieving; for example, they might back off as they had wanted distance and space, or equally they might be there all the time 'helping' as they had wanted more support.

What I expect is coming for me in the future, is a sense of better acceptance of the reality of life now, of adjustment. I am not sure whether I expect not to be grieving forever, but I do feel less 'broken' and am aware that life is different, it will never feel the same normal again that it was – that would require an act of raising the dead. What I do feel now is calmer, less manic. I don't know what the end of grief looks like; although some days I think I have reached it because I can think about Dad or my grandparents without feeling like I need to put up a protective barrier to stop the outpouring of uncontrollable emotion.

But I do still get upset. I still hate that he is not here to ask things or that he will not get to teach his grandchildren his wealth of experience and knowledge, his values and the importance of having fun that managed to get across to my siblings and I. These feelings of regret are not as intense nor do they last as long as they did before.

Many people I have spoken to say they it still hurts on some days, even decades later, and even if their person was elderly and their death was less unexpected.

I expect this process to continue and that, eventually, I will be able to sit with my memory of him and channel what he taught us and pass it on. I expect that I will always miss him but that, as I get further away that the pain will lessen each time the wound is knocked.

I know for you reading this now, at the beginning of your pain and upheaval, you do not want to think about this and maybe even resent that I have managed this. It's possible you are seeking a similar sense of moving on, or conversely that you cannot think of anything worse. It may seem that the concept feels like you have betrayed your loved one and have left them behind.

But it has taken me years and lots of help (from professionals and keen amateurs) to get to this point.

The hole that has been left by the grief will, over time, get gradually smaller and you will learn how to navigate around it, but certain events and situations will aggravate the boundaries and the hole will feel like it has gotten bigger again.

I expect to have learnt from this horrible – just horrible – life-changing and challenging time and hope that if I were ever starting this process again that I would be able to recognise my behaviour better. I would expect to be a little easier and kinder to myself.

I do know that you cannot do what others expect, you have to do what feels best for you. There is no right or wrong way to grieve, and not everyone or even many people will understand what you are going through or feeling and the difficulties you have overcome.

By expecting certain events to be difficult, I think you can equip and brace yourself. That is not to say it will not be painful, but it will hopefully reduce the surprise, because if you expect and anticipate that your feelings of grief will return, then hopefully they will do less damage when they do.

Quotes and poems

I know you sleep in heaven

> I know you sleep in heaven,
> And up there dream of me.
> Waiting there for those you love,
> Until together we will be.
> I know that you're not lonely,
> In company of angels above.
> Watching over and protecting,
> Those you left behind. – Dave Hedges

'Deep grief sometimes is almost like a specific location, a co-ordinate on a map of time. When you are standing in that forest of sorrow, you cannot imagine that you could ever find your way to a better place. But if someone can assure you that they themselves have stood in that same place, and now have moved on, sometimes this will bring hope' – Elizabeth Gilbert, *Eat, Pray, Love*

CHAPTER 6

Things That Made Me
Feel Better

Something that was a great help to me was the realisation, the acceptance, that there is no right or wrong way to grieve, and that it is perfectly fine for you to do whatever makes you feel a little more comfortable with the pain of your loss, the gaping hole you will feel in your life and body.

It is hard to talk about a death and the impact it has on you until you have had time to accept and comprehend some of it, especially so soon after it has happened. I think one of the first and strongest things you feel is shock, and with that an incomprehension simply that the person was here – and now they are not. You will probably think, 'How can this be?'

Although it can be difficult to talk about the death, it can be comforting and familiar to talk about the person and to share memories. I always enjoyed this, even if it did usually lead to an outburst of emotion, as I found it soothing and think it must go some way to helping you heal.

Do not try to accept it before you are ready. You will be trying to feel something you simply cannot or to do something that is as yet beyond you. I suppose you could say, you need to accept that one day you will accept it.

Some days you might feel philosophical but on others you may be frustrated, angry or heartbroken. That's OK, this process is yours and you are allowed to feel what you feel. Do not try to pretend for the sake of others or because it's what you think you should be doing.

Others may be comforted if they see you displaying your emotions, as they may have been hiding their feelings from you out of a sense of protecting you. Some people have to grieve privately, as they are upset and still working everything out, and sometimes you may be comforted and reassured by doing it with someone else – talking about the person who has died and their life.

It seems that grief needs a period of time. This period feels like a luxury, but it is not. It is a necessity. Let yourself have time.

Some people find that packing away everything that is associated to the deceased, both physically and metaphorically, is what gets them through. For whatever reason, they appear unable or unwilling to release any emotion and, if that is what works for them, then that is to be respected, even if personally that is not an approach you favour. I would imagine the last thing that they would want is to be regularly pushed and encouraged to 'unpack' these things. It may be something that they come back to decades later, if at all.

At some point in the first year after Dad and Granddad died, I felt I needed some help with what I was feeling, and through my GP I was referred to a counselling service. I found it was useful to have somewhere to go and talk with, to let off steam, as I seemed to be not only suffering from guilt and anger, but we had family issues too.

I personally have found counselling incredibly helpful and found it really valuable to have a safe space where I could cry or be angry without thinking that I had to edit my behaviour to protect someone else's feelings. It is a chance to talk to someone who is a trained professional, who is neutral. Sometimes people can try to make you feel better, and make themselves feel useful, by telling you silly titbits or repeating greetings-card aphorisms.

Retrospectively, I can appreciate now that around this time I did blow comments and conversations out of proportion, as my brain was muddled and my heart was hurting. I was at the same time trying so hard to control my anger and pain. It seemed I had lost the ability to listen and reason properly. I would perceive the most benign of comments as being extremely unfair and judgemental.

I felt the need to write things down – whether they were what I was thinking or feeling, or specific memories – and to gather memorable items to try and maintain a strong connection to my family so I did not forget them. I think I had a fear that I would forget as time passed. It seemed important to remember all the little things, the weird habits that made the person I loved who they were. For example, how my dad would wiggle a pen over the page before starting to write, as if he were getting it warmed up – or how he used to annoy me with the noise he made while eating toast!!

I needed things that would give me comfort and found great contentment in looking at old photographs, so I made a collage of my favourites, and the rest that I couldn't part with, I mounted in a scrapbook. I wrote down memories of places we had been on holidays and experiences we had enjoyed, and put everything in a box with other memorable items.

Sometimes, it was the most surprising and silly things that I kept. I found a travel book for somewhere I was about to visit on the bookshelf. In it was a little note that was in Dad's handwriting, I was upset as I wasn't expecting to find it – I either didn't realise or had forgotten that he had visited this place and had seen the things I was looking forward to seeing. Also, it was a reminder I was not going to see his handwriting again on new messages. I even kept another note I found, a phone message that he had taken from a man who was sorting out my pension; it was a very dull, everyday phone message but it was in his funny, little scribble, and I realised I was never going to get another handwritten message from him again.

In my scrapbook, I've also got birthday cards, postcards and just about anything that holds a memory that I can go back to when I feel the need. Over time, I have visited the box less and less, but it remains a comfort just to know it is there.

Music is such a strong trigger for many different emotions in people, as certain songs seem to fit the situation you might find yourself in or the way you were feeling.

Even now, when I hear some of the songs that were on the radio when the members of my family died, I can remember or even experience again those emotions that I had at the time, as the lyrics take on a new meaning and remind me of the person I am missing. Sometimes, even hearing a song by an artist who you know they enjoyed listening to will make you think of them.

I can remember having a sudden realisation, a moment of severe emptiness, while driving in a particular place, a memory of how I felt when I drove down the same road shortly after Dad had died. Sometimes, hearing some of the songs that were on the radio at the time will either upset me and I'll have a little teary moment, or I will feel a sense of comfort like someone is just rubbing my shoulder, giving me a hug or stroking my heart, as it has an unexpected, unsettled flutter.

A great comfort to me was my family, particularly my brothers, as he was their dad too, so we all understood the relationship.

However, spending time with my mum was great too, it was very different, but we encouraged and cheered each other up a little bit. It was something of a balancing act, a give and take of one of us supporting the other, depending on who was feeling the more down or upset. Sometimes, we just felt stronger together, particularly in the weeks and months after Dad and Granddad died. I felt I only wanted to be with my family as they understood my pain more than others could, I didn't need to explain anything to them, we could just 'be' and spend time together. I found that I tended to move away from people who didn't understand, as I felt self-conscious.

It was invaluable to have 'safe' people who understood, who had similar feelings, and I always feel incredibly lucky that I had my brothers and my mum around, that we could support each other. It must be so much harder for people who do not have someone to share those experiences with; people have told me how isolated they felt when their parents have died, as they had no siblings or family to share things with; plus, they had the challenge and responsibility of organising everything around the funeral and sorting out their belongings, as it falls only on them.

One of the things that I took great comfort in at the funerals for my dad and grandparents was spending time talking to family and friends and hearing stories that I had not heard before. It gave me a snapshot of the times in which they grew up, or I learned something I had not known before. It was as if I were getting to know them better rather than losing them. One of the most satisfying and lovely things about talking to these people (some of whom had known my relatives for years, since they were young adults) was hearing about how they had behaved, the things they had done, what had driven and inspired them or their attitude towards other people or towards work. Although of course they are family and there is bound to be some degree of identification, recognising in myself traits I was hearing about was wonderful. I suppose I had only ever seen them as parent or grandparent and had never really thought about who they were, or why they were the way they were – what had served to form their character. It felt as if the bond between us was somehow strengthened and I understood them better. It was as though, in some ways, they were not gone, as I could see them and their traits in me and my brothers, and even my own daughter.

After my dad died, I wanted to organise events to benefit a charity that is working to find a cure, or better treatments, for the leukaemia that killed him. Leukaemia Research, now called Bloodwise, is a charity that has been devoted to finding a cure for blood cancers since 1960. It is, to me of course, a phenomenal organisation which is determined to find a cure or cures for this terrible disease in order to prevent fewer families in the future from suffering loss as a result of it.

Although in part, organising events was a distraction and an aspect of the manic behaviour I had clearly developed to make it feel as if I had a purpose, it was also something I genuinely enjoyed. I felt I did have a purpose, it gave me something else to focus on, but this was I suppose also both good and bad; it is not unheard of for someone who has been bereaved to throw themselves into organising events or some other pursuit which keeps them busy. But, along with the distraction, it also meant I ultimately was delayed in processing and dealing with the grief.

However, it was lovely to have the support of people who knew and loved both my dad and our family, and gave us another opportunity to come together, celebrate and have fun.

Visit www.cuddleamemorybook.com to get useful suggestions and ideas on how to organise a charity event.

It always made me feel better to do things that I had enjoyed with them, as it made me feel closer to them, and in some way as though I had not let them go by letting go of the family traditions and interests we had shared.

It would help to feel connected to them; I would see friendly and familiar faces, and places. I would be able to more easily think about the times we had enjoyed together. It would also highlight our similarities and that was like they were giving me a little 'family' hug.

But I can appreciate that in some cases the memories and associations are too painful for some to cope with when they are in an environment they enjoyed together, as it is a harsh reality and can serve to highlight the new reality that they are no longer here – so those still here might feel more conspicuous and vulnerable.

There is a flip side to over indulging in the environments where you might feel they are closest, in that it can become all too easy to, in some sense, fantasise that they are still here and not really gone. This can fuel the denial of any change of circumstance. As much as, deep down, you will know the truth, the delay in truly accepting it will probably make it more painful and a new shock each time the reality has to be acknowledged.

Quite near the beginning, I needed time to myself, not talking to anybody. I think I was still in shock and I found it so hard to talk to people and deal with their expectations of my grief and of me, of what I was doing and how I was coping. Some people might have thought that just sitting and crying might help me, but I thought I was getting on with life and that was helping instead. I couldn't merely 'sit and stare at the four walls'.

People said to me at the time, and have done so since, that I didn't really cry that much early on after my dad had died. I did cry, but it would often need to be triggered to allow me to release it. Watching TV or listening to music, something would strike a chord, and that would set me off. I felt either very busy or very drained and never in between, so if I was sitting I would watch shows and films that were very benign and easy to watch, as I didn't have the concentration for anything that needed to be engaged with, such as books or reading of any kind.

I got into a few TV series, such as Grey's Anatomy, and became very attached to and invested in characters and storylines, as their experiences became an emotional outlet. I used it to zone out of myself and achieve numbness from my own thoughts and pain. I channelled everything into a fantasy world where I cared more about the characters than myself. I was comforted by this distraction and could for a time forget about the pain of losing my family members.

A few years later, when such characters left or the series ended I felt bereft, probably because I had invested a lot emotionally; this programme had been a comfort and an outlet for my grief, and I had started feeling some of the pain from that time again.

In the time after my dad's death, I needed things that distracted me, so I kept quite busy going to work, going out and seeing people, or planning outings and events.

I felt the need to keep doing things to make me feel alive, that I needed to make my life feel like it had a purpose. I felt I wanted to do things that would make my dad proud – that his life had purpose and to keep his memory alive.

Because I went back to work very soon after my dad died, on most days I had to work hard to put on a 'game face' – an Americanism which I understand to mean displaying the bravery you do not necessarily believe you have in order to get through the day. I became so used to putting my emotions in a box so that I could cope with a day at work that I found it hard to let them out again when I was not at work. I needed other things to trigger an outlet for my grief and emotions – I did a lot of crying while driving and had the radio on, even now, I still know which albums and individual tracks I listened to at the time, and to which I still have a strong emotional connection.

I actually, perhaps oddly, found crying as a result of another stimulus quite cathartic. It really helped me to switch off my 'game face' and just be who I was – vulnerable because I was involved and invested in someone else's pain, the pain of 'lost love' song lyrics, which was representative of my own pain. I did not know what my pain looked and felt like, so I guess I hijacked that from other people, even if they were characters from TV programmes, heartache from songs or stories from movies.

An event or situation that I might have found upsetting before, such as a TV programme or even an advertisement, would be so much more powerful; perhaps simply as an exaggeration of what it might always have done - but now it was a clear outlet for grief, and I felt if I could achieve 'quality crying', I might feel better

After organising the fundraising events, in the following year I set myself a challenge that every month I was going to do something I had never done before. I made the effort to do some of those little things you always mean to get around to – visit that art gallery or museum, learn how to make the best cupcakes, go to a football match, etc.

I think this also gave me a sense of purpose, in overcoming these mini-challenges, because life is still for living, and I felt like I needed to make the most of every opportunity that I could. Plus, it gave me something to look forward to and get excited about.

Another thing that helped me was carrying on doing things that I used to enjoy with Dad and my family, as it made me feel close to him or that he was not 'gone'. It was comforting and sometimes made me feel nothing had really changed, as I had the memories of him. Then sometimes, it could actually highlight the fact that he was really not here, which could be painful.

Before my dad died, he had started to teach me to fly a hot air balloon – he had learnt a few years before he became ill – and I decided I wanted to continue this. It was something I had always wanted to do, it made me feel close to him and kept his memory and our hobby alive. I felt determined to carry on with life and plans we had made.

The reality of trying to achieve this was different than I had hoped for, as it was incredibly painful, emotionally, very bittersweet, and it required a lot of time and concentration that I just was not always capable of. There was also the problem that, when I had a new teacher, I could not help but think, 'Dad's teaching style would have been different and better for me.' I struggled to adjust and accept that I needed to find a new approach to this hobby to enjoy it again; having to learn with someone else took a bit of the fun out, and that made it harder still.

I joined a few groups on social media for grief and bereavement and would browse through looking at the poems, quotes and other words of wisdom. I felt they were talking to me and that they really seemed to voice what I was struggling with. I could relate to most of them to varying degrees. It was almost like they were the things I struggled to say but also comforting that I had something to identify with or someone could identify with me, or that I was not the only or first person to have these feelings and frustrations. I have included some of the ones that really touched me throughout this book in case you felt the same.

When I found something or some situation tough, wherever possible I looked for a solution to make myself feel better. In the case of anniversaries such as Father's Day and Dad's birthday, I managed this by still buying him a card and writing in it what I wanted to say to him. It would then be put up in pride of place, next to his photo, for a while. When I decided to take them down, I burnt them and dug the ashes into the roots of a rose I bought in his memory. You will, I am sure, find your own way to deal, celebrate or remember them at these difficult times.

I think when you realise that the sad memories you have about the person who died do not eclipse the happy memories, that is when you will feel that you have cracked it. When you can hold those happy and sad memories side by side, enjoying the happy ones without dwelling on and constantly going over the sad ones, then that is really a sign that something has changed.

A Note on Counselling

A service where you work with a qualified practitioner, counselling offers a safe space, a one-to-one environment that allows you to express exactly what is on your mind, and how you are feeling without judgement, pre-conception or hidden agenda, and without risk of hurting or offending the other person. This service can be offered through a GP referral, in a private practice or through a charity. It is something that is also offered by hospices or respite care, and illness specific or general charities too.

Poems

Until We Meet Again

Those special memories of you,
will always bring a smile,
If only I could have you back,
For a little while.
Then we could sit and talk again,
just like we used to do,
You always meant so much to me,
and always will do too.
The fact that you're no longer here,
will always cause me pain.
But you're forever in my heart,
Until we meet again – Author unknown
Forever in Your Heart
Feel no guilt in laughter
She knows how much you care,
Feel no sorrow in a smile
That she's not here to share.
You cannot grieve forever

She would not want you to,
She'd hope that you would carry on
The way you always do.
So talk about the good times
And the ways you showed you cared,
The days you spent together
All the happiness you shared.
Let the memories surround you
A word someone might say,
Will suddenly recapture
A time, an hour, a day.
That brings her back as clearly
As though she was still here,
And fills you with the feelings
That say she's always near.
For if you keep those moments
You will never be apart,
And they will live forever
Safely locked within your heart .– Author unknown

CHAPTER 7

The Reality of Living Without Them

The long-term reality of not having somebody in your life is a juggling act. Some days you will feel and act fine and not think about them – or you will be able to do so without dissolving into tears. Other days you will feel just as devastated as you did on your most difficult days immediately after their death.

It is hard to accept that they are missing from your life, and they are missing important events in your family. You cannot help but miss them at such times and think about how much better the celebration would be if they were there with you. It is an elephant in the room. Sometimes, they will be acknowledged on such occasions, sometimes they won't – the occasion will still take place.

At some points, you can and will have waves of anger and resentment that they are not there, focused both on the person who has died and towards the people who are surrounded by seemingly all their loved ones at special events.

I think it is for you to find a way of making it feel as alright as possible. Everyone struggles and deals with it in their own way, but find a way that helps you acknowledge them on those days.

Consider taking a photo of them along with you, so you feel like they are there or if there is a baby due in the family, think about maybe using their name. If you are going to a family event, take one of their possessions with you, such as a tie or piece of jewellery, so that you can feel that, in some shape or form, they are included and are still there – that they still have some physical presence in what is going on.

Try not to rely on others to remember your pain and to make it feel better, as you might be disappointed, they might not feel it the same way you do.

Significant days that I find particularly difficult are birthdays, anniversaries, Christmas and days with both good and bad news, as they are days we would have shared as a family, but their absence seems greater somehow. I miss their presence, their insight and input, and they magnify the emotions of the day.

It is not only a case of somehow learning to live with it; it is about accepting it too, as you must in order for the pain to subside. At some point you will find a way, and you will, even though you might not want to.

You will feel like you are learning to walk or breathe all over again; I was happy for distractions and to stay active. I wanted to make my life feel it counted and therefore Dad's life counted too - I wanted to feel as though I were continuing to make him proud. Even six years later, I still think about what he would say about things, what he would think about what was going on, what advice he would give, what his contributions to a situation would be. Some days, I can imagine him with us, I can see the look on his face or the twinkle in his eye. Sometimes, that can be comforting, and other times it is still a reminder that he is not here, which can be painful.

Getting back to normal is something that is never going to happen, as life will never feel normal again, in terms of what 'normal' was.

There is what is nowadays termed a 'new normal', which you will need to accept.

As much as I can now function on a day-to-day basis without the constant pain that I had at the beginning, there is always an underlying feeling on some level that there is something missing, because there is one less person to ask for advice, there is one less person to give me a hug when I want one or wish me a happy birthday.

I think both the phrases 'back to normal' and 'time's a great healer' are not quite right; the best way I can describe it is I feel less broken than I did. That is not to say I do not find things funny anymore, that I don't love life or enjoy things I used to because I do. I did feel guilty for having fun or enjoying myself, but I don't anymore.

I love being with my family and, as much as I enjoy it, I am often aware that there is somebody missing, and I do not think that will ever change.

If I am honest, I'm not sure I want it to, because the reality of that would be that I would have to forget what it felt like to have Dad around. I do not want to forget that.

You or the situation will never be back to normal or better, but you will feel less broken and will find a new normal.

Bereavement is a bit like losing a limb, both are life-changing events. Some people never manage to adjust or get over it; some people sit around waiting for others to do everything for them,; while others successfully adapt and come back to feeling near to where they were before. Others still find something about the new situation is better than how life was before; it inspires them to do something they would never have done before, such as people going on to compete at the Paralympic Gamers.

I decided I was going to be honest when telling people about bereavement; with this in mind, I am pursuing a change of career, and am retraining as a counsellor. I also make memory bears, where I use fabrics with a special meaning to the customer to create a teddy bear so it can be enjoyed every time you need it. This can be, for example, the fabric from a favourite shirt that your loved one wore regularly; or perhaps a child's jumper or a Babygro that has been grown out of. They can form part of a bespoke, beautiful teddy bear.

As a special bonus, visit www.cuddleamemorybook.com for a money off voucher towards your own bespoke bear.

When you lose a grandparent, you might expect it a bit more, although it is still painful. Losing a parent was of course less expected and made me feel very vulnerable from above, you are now the top of the chain, if you like, and I felt unprotected and that my support had gone. I thought, 'How will I cope? Who will help and support me if my dad is no longer here to fill that role?'

I have said earlier that we, as a society, do not talk enough about death, and we talk even less about one really negative feeling that comes with it – guilt.

One of the hardest things when you lose somebody is getting used to the guilt; I do not think people expect to feel this when they lose a loved one.

I think guilt is one of the most difficult, almost overwhelming aspects of grief because it comes in so many different layers.

The guilt that you could have done more, that you should have done more, than what you did do – could you have done it differently? Could I have done more to get an earlier diagnosis? How should I have made the last few days more comfortable?

What could I have done to help them stay healthy? What could I have done to make them feel more loved?

The guilt that you should have shown them how much you cared more often.

The guilt that you did not tell them as much as you should have, and why didn't you? The guilt that you did not ask more questions, acquire more of their knowledge while you had the chance.

It is easy to you feel guilty and resentful of the fact you have unanswered questions, you might wish you had told them more that you loved them. Or they had told you they loved you. You might wish you had taken every opportunity that you were given to see and appreciate them, and for them to know how much you appreciated them. You might even feel guilty that you did not.

In retrospect, I did things to make memories of my dad when I wished I could have made more memories with him. I wanted to keep all my memories locked up in a box because I was so scared of losing them and forgetting him. I thought that if I forgot any memory of him then it would feel that he had gone a little bit further away.

When someone dies, you think about him or her all the time, so when you stop thinking about them so much you can feel like you are forgetting them. When I think back to before Dad died, I know I did not think about him every minute of every day but just had the comfort of knowing that he was there. It's strange, you go from not thinking about them when they are there, to thinking about them constantly when they are gone.

I think grief acts as an emotional exaggerator, it makes everything more difficult. Everything is harder to cope with and feels like a bigger drama because you are trying to deal with the pain of losing someone, trying to adjust and comprehend the new reality you now have. The pain of bereavement seems so all-consuming, your reactions to everyday problems or situations are out of proportion and are a reflection of the upheaval you are feeling.

Anything can be an emotional trigger – every song, book, TV programme, film and even magazine article takes on a new significance and reminds you somehow of the person you are missing – what they enjoyed or disliked, how they would have responded or reacted.

Getting 'back to normal' means being able to listen to a song without it being so painful, where it previously provoked a strong emotional reaction and had left you preoccupied with thoughts of that person or side-tracked from a task you were working on by the pain of not having them there.

Getting back to normal means no longer being distracted by the same whirl of alternating emotions that you had before. There might be a step towards acceptance, but there are still times when I feel angry and resentful, even if the reality is that those emotions do not change anything, they do not bring the person back. When this anger and resentment returns, I think you do in a way have to restart the process of acceptance again – and I think this does get easier with time. That does not mean you are not going to be upset or that it will not be painful; merely that you will, over time, feel less resentful of what you must accept.

My dad was always my voice of reason and, sometimes, as weird as it might sound, I wanted to share the experience of his death with him, to talk it over, get his views on it. He was always a calming influence, and I knew that if I could talk to him about it, I would feel better.

Grief can be so overwhelming. It feels like life is going on over your head and you are existing under a cloud, almost as though you have got all this stuff going on around you but you are not involved – you are in this 'grief bubble' and are going through the motions. It is not that you are not feeling or doing certain things, more that it is all on the outskirts. You are trying to get hold of it, but there is no shape or substance, you are not sure how to take hold of it. You need this space within your bubble to feel like normality is continuing, as that is how you are used to functioning, but there is pressure from all these new emotions on the outside of the bubble. The world out there has changed, you know emotions are there, but you just need to keep them at arm's length for a little while just until you sum up the mental and physical energy, and the courage, to deal with them. I think some people do not realise that the film of their bubble is delicate and one small thing can burst it, then all those thoughts and feelings come pouring in unexpectedly and absolutely floor you – only, it is not unexpected because they have always been there, and you have been working hard on how to control them. It is just at that point in time they have overwhelmed and incapacitated you.

When that bubble bursts, you will be floored. You cannot think straight, you can barely reason or function, and you find it difficult to be logical. You thought you were doing all of those things while you were in the bubble, but it's only later that you will see that that was not really you or how you would normally react to things.

If you are going through that process or any of this looks familiar, please just bear in mind that you could be overreacting to some events, or acting in an unusual or out of character way. Therefore, people's responses to you could be different; they might be hurt or offended, or could be surprised by what you do or say. This might lead you to feel guilty or possibly angry about it; it is important that people around you know this is not who you normally are. This is all completely normal, go easy on yourself, it will settle down.

The reality of getting back to normal will mean going back to work, socialising again, getting used to and adjusting to that gap in your life. This process will take as long as it takes, and that is different for everybody. What is hard is seeing people around you adjusting more quickly and you might feel like they are forgetting – you might not want them to.

I think in the beginning of grief, you are resentful of having to get back to normal. You are resentful that life has had to change because you were not ready for it, did not want it and it's hard having to accept that this has happened. Getting back to normal will mean that your thoughts will flow more smoothly, you will feel less frustrated and you can think in a straighter line.

The interesting or strange thing that I did realise after my dad died was how I felt about my own death, as morbid as this may seem. I realised I felt quite calm about it, had no fear or apprehension. I felt that it was a natural and inevitable process, and the only fearful part was the bit before; but death itself no longer felt strange and unknown, as then I knew that my dad would be there (wherever or whatever happens) to meet me, give me a hug and help me once again. This thought gave me comfort and really helped settle some unidentifiable, unsettling feelings.

Quotes and poems

'There are things that we don't want to happen but have to accept, things we don't want to know but have to learn, people we can't live without but have to let go.' – Nancy Stephan, (author)

CHAPTER 8

How to Support – What the Bereaved Need: Advice for Family and Friends

This will, in many respects, be as tough for you as it is for the person you are trying to support, as there is a strong likelihood that you will have also known the person they are grieving for.

This will probably mean that you are, to some degree, also grieving for the same person; this could get overlooked and/or forgotten by the bereaved person. For this, I can only sympathise and attempt to explain how and why this might happen.

When a death and bereavement have hit you hard and you are struggling, in my experience, it is hard to fully communicate how you are feeling, and the thoughts and emotions that are stirred up can preoccupy you to the extent that it can be hard to remember other people and keep in touch with what is going on around you.

Life feels like it is going on around you while you are merely existing in a bubble; you can see and to some extent interact with the outside world, but that is limited; the complete mess your head and heart are in means you become very forgetful.

Now, you may be feeling some of this yourself, and you may be having to shelve your feelings to enable you to help 'your person' – the bereaved person you are close to – get through this period. – how long it will take is dependent on them. My main messages to you are:

- They could be angry and resentful

- They could be taking risks, as they might not care about themselves. Part of them may want to be with their loved one, or else they are functioning on adrenaline and will therefore feel untouchable.

- There will be some strange behaviour, even euphoria, which could be in part due to tiredness and/or an uncertainty of knowing what else to feel.

- They have so many thoughts and feelings they cannot pick just one to express to you, so are likely to say, 'I am fine', having reached a plateau of coping as struggling to process thoughts and feelings.

- They will probably not want to ask for help.

- They could withdraw and/or retreat, as they feel they can no longer relate to you as your life appears to be perfect by comparison, and there is no way that you could relate to what they are feeling.

- They will be feeling several emotions within the space of an hour.

- They could be feeling confused and a bit lost.

- They will find it tough to concentrate, so might lose patience or energy halfway through a task and therefore abandon it. There could be days when they are unable to do much more than get out of bed and others when they are happy to be busy doing lots of things, and then perhaps a few days of nothing.

- They might want to hibernate.

- They will be tired as they may not be sleeping, or tired and want to do nothing else but sleep; the emotions can feel so overwhelming that they weigh you down, or the brain continues to whirl while in bed, making sleep difficult.

- They could be frustrated with seemingly everything and everyone – this could well be displaced, as above; this frustration could be an outlet for the feelings, such as resentment, they are having.

- You can't make someone feel or deal with something they are not ready to deal with. Try to support and encourage rather than push or force, as it will do more harm than good.

- Don't take anything too personally. You will probably act as someone who some misplaced emotions are 'vented' at, but do not be too disheartened as this could be that they feel supported enough by you to do so.

- Everyone grieves differently; therefore, there is no right or wrong way to do it.

- You may feel for a while that the relationship becomes a bit one-way. Try to offer open communication; they might not 'do' subtle, so you may just have to be gently honest.

- Be aware that they will not be logical or rational; expect outbursts of anger. It may seem out of proportion, as it may not even be about the situation at hand. It may start there but escalate because they are grieving and in pain. They may be snappy as they are preoccupied with the mix of emotions and thoughts they are trying to organise and process.

- They may also be really tired. Any outbursts are not

personal to you; if they are being offensive to you then that needs to be addressed, but if it is a strong reaction it could be about something else. Do not forget the strength of any reaction is fuelled with grief.

They want more than anything else to be able to talk to the person who has died. Hold them and ask them something, even if it is just for an hour.

One of the hardest things when you lose somebody close to you is the reactions to you of other people, and I think the closer you are to the person who has died, the tougher the grief you feel; therefore, the more difficult people might find it to respond and interact with you.

I'm sure we have all been in a situation where somebody we know has had a family bereavement, and you might feel awkward because you do not know what to say, what not to say or how to interact with them, as you do not want to risk upsetting them.

Now I have been on the other side, I hope I understand a little bit better. I now find it is easier to actually talk to someone who has suffered a bereavement, and I now know what I would want people to say if I were in their situation.

I think tip-toeing around the situation or treading on eggshells can be frustrating. I'm sure it is well intentioned, but I think the best option for you is just to be honest, direct and speak from the heart. You don't know how that person is going to be feeling that day.

I think this social awkwardness is something that can be said of many situations in life, not just around death. Maybe it's a British problem!

Even a few days after my dad died, I felt fine and I could talk and laugh about him without getting upset, whereas a few months later on I was struggling. I could tear up at the slightest thing, just when everybody else seemed to be thinking that I was over the worst of it because I had been so OK, so 'normal', soon after it had happened.

Therefore, it is better not to second-guess what the other person might be thinking or wanting you to say. Just saying what you want to, as neutrally as possible, is probably what that person wants to hear.

I had a colleague once ask me for some advice when her friend had lost her mum. My colleague said, 'I don't know what to say to her,' as the friend still wanted to continue with their plan to go out and socialise, and this made my colleague uncomfortable. 'It seems wrong going out, she's just lost her mum,' my colleague said.

I advised her that her friend probably really wanted to continue as planned, as she might not know what else to do. It was not for my colleague to make a decision about what her friend wanted, needed or should be doing.

I also advised her to be prepared for the plan to change if her friend changed her mind, that her friend was probably still in shock and that the best thing she could say to her would be, 'Sorry to hear about your mum, that must be absolutely awful. I can't imagine what you're going through.'

Then, 'I am happy to listen if you want to talk, but if you would rather not talk about it then I can happily talk about our usual topics and gossip.'

And finally, 'If at any stage, you feel you want to change the subject and talk about your mum then please feel free to do so.'

You might think that all the person would want to do is talk about the loved one and how much they are struggling, but the reality is more nuanced. They are of course likely to be heartbroken and perhaps even in shock, and what they feel cannot always be articulated at that moment. They could just be feeling numb and not even begun to work out how they are going to comprehend all of these emotions and feelings, let alone think about the changes or adjustments in their life that might lie ahead. They could be happy to have a distraction or sense that everything is OK. They are carrying on.

But the opposite is also true. It may be that it is hard to talk about the person they have lost. having been ill or them dying, that they may be missing them and the situation is too overwhelming to think about, but they are comforted by talking about their memories and stories as it makes the deceased still feel close by.

Let them guide you.

When asked how to behave, what to do around someone who is grieving or what to say when seeing them, I try to explain that at the beginning they may be in shock or they may dissolve into tears extremely easily; therefore, I feel the best and safest way to communicate with someone in this situation is to be honest and direct.

It may make you uncomfortable, but at least everyone knows where they are. There is less of a chance of misunderstanding and they will not notice that you might feel awkward – they are probably going to be too distracted. However, they will be grateful for your honesty.

Try saying, 'I'm sorry to hear x has died'; or, 'I'm sorry to hear about your sad news, that sounds dreadful'; and then, 'Although I can only imagine what you must be going through, I am here for you. Feel free to contact me or send me a text, or I could call you.'

It is also important to make it clear that, if they do not want to talk about it, you will be happy to continue to be there for them and talk about the usual topics of conversation. Also, suggest that if at any time they do want to bring it up and talk about it, that is fine too.

It might also be helpful to ask them about the person who has died, they may find comfort in visiting memories. Ask them, 'What is your favourite memory?' 'What was their favourite joke?' 'Is there anywhere you would like to visit that you enjoyed together?'

Be clear to change the subject if that is what they desire.

Ask them, 'I know you say you are fine – is that because you want me to behave as we always have and not to give you any special treatment?'

If you struggle to be around them because you find it too upsetting yourself, then surely it is best to say that rather than them feeling abandoned. They might feel even worse simply because of the grief they are feeling.

You could even try setting up a 'safe' word – a code word between you so that if they seem quiet, you know that they may or may not want to talk about it. You could find saying a code word easier than them attempting to say, 'I am feeling a bit upset and want some time,' or, 'Please respect my request that I need five minutes on my own.'

By having a short, benign phrase, they can quickly and easily have a moment to themselves. Here are some suggestions:

Jumper – which could mean, 'I do not want to talk, but I am struggling so please give me hug. I may open up when feeling supported and less overwhelmed.'

Kit-Kat – 'Please give me a five-minute break to compose myself. I cannot cope with this situation right now, but maybe after a cup of tea I'll be fine.'

Umbrella – 'Please cover for me. I need some space.'

Sofa – 'Please just sit with me and talk about any old distracting gossip.'

Hand grenade – 'I am about to explode. I cannot necessarily explain why, but I can feel a rise of rage or emotions.'

I think most people when dealing with the shock of a death, feel so unfamiliar with their life and how it has changed, that what they will need from you is to be able to rely on the consistency of your friendship and support. As everyone deal and adjusts in their own way, unless your friend is easily able to communicate what they are feeling, then you will, for the most part, have to imagine what they are going through – they will find it difficult to put it into words. With this in mind, what will hold them is you giving them what is familiar, or normal, to them.

Do not be scared of asking how they are feeling, they may or may not tell you, or they may not be able to tell you. Some people feel like they do not want to ask for fear of upsetting the person grieving, but you will not be reminding them of anything. They know all too well what the reality is and are probably trying to ignore or struggling to forget. This does not mean they will not appreciate you asking them how they are feeling.

Do not be offended, if you feel like you want to offer advice and they do not want to hear it. They may seek your company and support but not always for a 'deep and meaningful' conversation. They might just want a cup of tea, a hug or a shoulder to cry on and just a chance to talk about the person they are missing, rather than run through their emotions. A simple chat could be just what they need to make them feel better.

Stay strong, they may need someone to be around who they can let it all out and vent to, as situations escalate and they can become sensitive and begin overreacting.

It may be difficult for them to talk to other family members, and their actions at this particularly difficult time can bring up some strong reactions, get on their nerves and annoy them. This may seem like an overreaction to you, but to them it will be real and could be fuelled by a sense of displaced injustice. They may just need you to be a sounding board, as they are not necessarily looking for solutions; once they have had a chance to let off steam about a situation and calmed down, they may be able to see it with a different perspective.

Try not to take any negativity towards you personally; it is impossible for the bereaved person to be angry with the person who has died. They love and miss them too much to have negative feelings towards them, but negative feelings they are experiencing can therefore be directed at other people and brought to bear on situations that are still around them.

Be patient, if you have offered open-ended help or a shoulder to cry on, I am sure they will take you up on the offer eventually, although they might just need reminding after a few weeks or a month. They may think you have 'moved on', as life does, but they will be stuck where they were and because time has passed they might be too nervous to ask for help.

Ask about the person they are missing. They will probably find it easier to talk about and want to tell you about the things they loved about them – memories of fun and holidays, their idiosyncrasies or even things that annoyed them. They will need someone new to share with what they used to share and reminisce about with their loved one.

If you know they are sorting through belongings, why not go round with some biscuits and bags for a charity shop donation? It is easy to think they will be fine and ready to do go through things belonging to the person they have lost, but I think it is difficult to do so without scratching the 'wound', to an extent re-opening the grief they have suffered. It helps to have someone to share the memory with. Your role can be to help to decide whether something is worth keeping or is OK to let go of.

Find an alternative way of getting across what you might struggle to say; if you want to just let someone know you are thinking of them, you can send a card – many greetings cards are blank and are so suitable for any occasion. It could be of an ocean view, a cute animal or even just a funny picture, just letting someone know they are in your thoughts can be very helpful and help to open communication with them. It is a gentle way to remind someone that you are there, as people often find it difficult to ask for help. It can make us uncomfortable. No one wants to feel like they are being needy or a burden, and they may not even know they need help, lesser still what form that may take.

You might have to give a lot and be rejected, but know that it is not you or your fault. It is probably more likely to be them. They may not be ready or know how to accept the support you are offering, but I am sure they will feel better just to know you are there and thinking of them.

I am sure you have thought about how you would react or behave if you were in their situation. You will probably try and offer what you think you would like, and you of course know your friend and how they respond and interact with you and others. Be mindful that a close bereavement to some extent changes them and they may act or behave in a way you do not recognise, which can be really difficult and testing. They do need and will continue to need you, even if they say or imply that they do not; it just may no longer be in a way that is familiar or usual for you both.

Every person reacts differently with grief, and this is as personal as a fingerprint. No one thing will suit two people, some may not want to hear wise words, or clichés, while some might like them and feel they are helpful. I am not suggesting that you behave in a way that is unnatural, but there may be some changes to your dialogue and interaction. Sometimes, in such a situation people will say things they would not otherwise when they are uncomfortable and don't know what to say.

Make a note in your diary for anniversaries, especially for the first few years, as these are hard; you may think they have forgotten, but I am sure that they have not. It is common for people with more distance not to remember the actual dates of events – the birthday of the person who has died, for example – and this is a time those nearest will have all their original feelings stirred up and will be struggling. Any acknowledgement I am sure will be appreciated, that you are thinking about them on what is a tough day. If after a few years they have more of a handle on it, at least they know you remembered. I cannot imagine someone being ungrateful to thoughtfulness or a message or call.

Be mindful of the possibility that any happy occasion could be tinged with sadness, as it will highlight that they are no longer here to share it. This is not to say their happiness is not genuine but that at some point during the day they may be feeling emotional.

Other things that might help them is if they feel they want to organise a memorial or a fundraising event, this can provide a real focus. The grief can really be motivating for them, and although this will feel positive, it will be tricky and stir up feelings, as it is a reminder that they are not here anymore. Fundraising requires a lot of support so it is always lovely to have someone to share that with.

If organising an event does not feel like something that would help, then maybe supporting an event to raise money or awareness would be better, especially if their person died of a particular illness or were supported by the work of a charity. This feeling of giving something back or raising awareness (perhaps helping to reduce the numbers of other people suffering as they have) can be very rewarding and soothing. Attending an event for an organisation that was supported by the deceased can help to feel like their passion and beliefs are being continued.

For testimonials and advice from friends and family who tried to support me through this time, visit www.cuddleamemorybook. com

Quotes and poems

Speak Their Name
Someone I love has gone away
And life is not the same,
The greatest gift that you can give
Is just to speak their name
I need to hear the stories
And the tales of days gone past,
I need for you to understand
These memories must last.
We cannot make more memories,
Since they're no longer here,
So when you speak of them to me,
It's music to my ear – Out of the ashes (website, author unlisted)

'Grief lasts longer than sympathy, which is one of the tragedies of the grieving' – Elizabeth McCracken, (writer)

'If you know someone who has lost a child, and you're afraid to mention them because you think you might make them sad by reminding them that they died – you're not reminding them. They didn't forget they died. What you're reminding them of is that you remembered that they lived, and... that is a great gift.' – Elizabeth Edwards, (writer)

'People keep telling me that life goes on, but, to me, that's the saddest part.' – Author unknown

'Our most difficult task as a friend is to offer understanding when we don't understand.' – Robert Brault, (writer)

'If ever there is tomorrow when we're not together... there is something you must always remember. You are braver than you believe, stronger than you seem, and smarter than you think. But the most important thing is, even if we're apart... I'll always be with you.' – A.A. Milne, (writer)

CHAPTER 9

Religion

The impartial, logical and rational part of us would probably say that when somebody dies, their body has ceased to live too, and that is it – the end. But equally, logic is an entirely human desire to attempt to understand and make sense of what has happened and what will happen in future. For this reason and over hundreds of years, we have attempted to give meaning to the sense of grief and loss, via concepts such as afterlife, spirits and spirituality, and heaven and hell.

For generations, religion has served to give comfort and provide answers and helped millions of people who are suffering from their grief and loss.

Of course, millions of people believe in their god and have faith, and I feel sure that in times of extreme stress, such as grief, a lot more people go looking for a religion. Some people research several religions, different from the one they grew up with, and there can be aspects of different faiths that can offer comfort and help someone to rationalise, reason and understand what has happened.

Religion can provide a way to help people to make sense of life, particularly when their life seems unfair – such as at times of grief and suffering.

Even if it is not a religion that you personally believe in, there can be facets of the theory and practice that can assist and be attractive. After all, those who do believe in a religion have a framework to follow during the process of grief; by having this framework, you have a sense of containment, something to set limits of what you might be feeling and thinking about.

If you believe in reincarnation, ultimately you do not have the same feeling of loss that the loved one has gone forever – that person can be anywhere; for instance, a bird singing in a tree as you walk past.

Other than just death and grief, learning about different faiths is important in terms of increasing our understanding of other cultures.

It may also be of comfort while grieving, as one aspect in a religion may help you to come to an understanding of someone else's wishes that are different from your own. For example, a person's wish to be cremated may jar with those of other family members; whereas Sikhs, for example, believe that the body is merely clothing for the soul, and that cremation is a means to release it. Sikhism also discourages gravestones and memorials; the body is not the true nature of the person, that is the spirit, which continues. From this point of view, concerns over cremation or burial could appear less relevant.

What is important is that people in every religion have found that at the funeral service, being able to show their grief formally assisted them in coping with or getting over their loss.

Here are some explanatory paragraphs about religions, in alphabetical order.

Buddhism

Buddhists are always encouraged to remember the impermanence of life; in the teachings of the Buddha, all of us will pass away eventually as part of the cycle of birth, old age and death. Of course, we will all cherish and wish to hold on to life, but it is important to remember that life is not permanent.

In Buddhism, death is not the end of life, it is merely the end of the body that we inhabit in this life – the soul will seek out through the need of attachment a new body to inhabit. All of life and death is a continuous cycle, called Samsara.

Through good actions, such as ethical conduct, and by developing concentration and wisdom, Buddhists hope to either gain enlightenment or to ensure a better future for themselves. These good actions are set out in the Eightfold Path, a way of living, which includes right speech, right livelihood and right concentration. Where and how they will be born, or born again, is the result of karma, the positive and negative actions of prior existence. Being reborn as a human being provides an opportunity to work towards escaping this cycle of Samsara, or death and rebirth, by achieving enlightenment or Nirvana.

Buddhism also teaches that the only thing that can help us at the time of death is our mental and spiritual development; the only thing that goes with us to the next life is our mind, along with its positive or negative karmic imprints. Wealth, possessions or position can provide no help to us, and neither can friends or relatives, as they cannot prevent death or accompany us to the next life. Therefore, it is important to work at being a better person, to strive to ripen our inner potential at all times, as we do not know when death will happen.

In Tibetan Buddhism, there is also the Tibetan Book of the Dead, a guide for a dying person, to try and ensure a positive outcome and to help them through what are called the Bardo States, states between death and rebirth.

Buddhist teachings hold that the final moment of consciousness is paramount, the most important of all. If a loved one is in hospital and the prognosis is grim, the family should call in a Buddhist priest to pray for the loved one so that, at the final moment, the right state of mind has been generated within the person and they can find their way into a higher state of rebirth as they leave their present life.

In such a scenario, medical staff and family members should not touch the body until at least three and as many as eight hours have passed since breathing stopped, as it is believed the spirit of the person will linger on and can be affected by what happens.

It is important that the body is treated gently and with respect. The Buddhist priest can help the spirit continue its journey calmly to higher states, and not causing the spirit to becoming angry and confused, which may make it more likely to be reborn into the lower realms of existence. The length of the actual period of mourning can vary, according to the particular traditions of the school or sect of Buddhism that is followed and the circumstances of the family.

Many have an intense period of mourning, involving chants, prayers and other rituals in the family home. It is common for such rituals to take place on the seventh, 49th and 100th days after the death. Others choose the seventh day, then three months and one year, but what is common is they are simple services allowing the family and friends of the deceased to come together and share their remembrance and a spiritual experience.

Christianity

Blessed are those who mourn, for they shall be comforted. (Matthew, 5:4)

I am the resurrection and the life. (John, 11:25)

Although there are myriad branches of Christianity, a central tenet is the belief in resurrection, as Christ was resurrected. Once the day of judgement arrives, they will be judged for their sins and bound for either heaven or hell.

In Christian theology, spiritual death is separation from God, which happens via sin – which entered the world through the fall of man; Adam and Eve's regrettable moment with the apple in the Garden of Eden. People are reconciled with God through the atoning sacrifice of Jesus Christ.

Spiritual death is related to but distinct from physical death and the so-called second or eternal death. According to the doctrine of original sin, all people are born with a sinful nature and thereby spiritually dead; being separated from God. Christians believe that because Christ defeated sin and death, those who have faith in him are made spiritually alive. Physical death is the separation of the spirit – the soul – from the body. For most Christians, physical death means the beginning of eternal life in the presence of God. According to Protestants, the unbeliever's physical death is followed by the second death (or eternal death and suffering).

Members of The Church of Jesus Christ of Latter-day Saints, often called Mormons, make a distinction between two types of spiritual death; first, a 'temporal separation' and second, a 'spiritual separation' from God. The first is a physical separation from God the Father, which was caused by the, as mentioned earlier, regrettable episode between Adam and Eve. Because of their choice, all their descendants are born into a fallen world that is physically separated from God's presence.

This separation is necessary so that individuals can be tested to see whether they will continue to be obedient even when not in God's presence – it is overcome unconditionally when all people return to God's physical presence for the judgment.

The second, spiritual separation from God's spirit or influence, which is caused by individual sins; when we sin we alienate ourselves from the influence of the Holy Ghost, God's spiritual presence. This is seen as being a completely unnecessary separation, as it only serves to impede our personal growth and ability to develop Godly attributes. Its resolution is started via baptism, after which a person receives the gift of the Holy Ghost. It is only overcome on the conditions of faith and repentance.

Christians believe there is an afterlife. Although the body dies and is buried or cremated, they believe that their soul lives on and is raised to new life by God.

Their belief that Jesus rose from the dead three days after his death gives Christians hope that if they follow Jesus's teaching and accept him as their Lord and Saviour, then this new resurrection life awaits them. By being born as a human being (the incarnation), and then dying on the cross, Jesus made this life after death possible for all.

Christians believe that God is just and fair, and so cannot let evil go unpunished. Most believe in the idea of judgement after death, and that God will treat people in the afterlife according to how they lived their life on earth.

Although heaven is often mentioned in the Bible, it is rarely described. Christians therefore have very different ideas about it. Some believe that heaven is a physical place where their body goes after death. Others believe that it is their soul that lives on, and that heaven is a state of that being united with God.

The Bible is even less specific about hell, and Christians have very different ideas about this too. Some Christians believe that hell is a place of suffering, the fiery place full of demons of conventional representation, and a state of separation from God. Others, perhaps even most Christians, believe that hell is a spiritual state of being separated from God for eternity.

Some Christians, including Roman Catholics, believe in purgatory. This is an in-between state for the majority of people of waiting for heaven, a time of cleansing from sin and preparing for heaven.

Many Christians believe that there is a place in the Kingdom of God for members of other faiths, and for many who have not even believed in God on earth but have carried out the will of God on many occasions, without knowing it.

Some Christians believe in the Second Coming, the return of Jesus Christ from heaven to earth, and that this will herald the general resurrection of the dead, the last judgement of the dead and the living, and the full establishment of the Kingdom of God on earth.

Each branch of Christianity has its own customs and practices around death; for example, Catholics often have an open coffin before the funeral, and so people can pay their respects and actually see the person who has died. This is less common in other forms of Christianity.

Both burial and cremation form part of Christian funeral services, and whichever is chosen is now a decision for the family, or sometimes the person who has died had been able to let people know their wishes beforehand.

Unlike other faiths, there is less emphasis on defined mourning periods or religious acts that must be carried out.

Hinduism

One of the largest religions in the world, by some estimates there are one billion Hindus worldwide. These are mainly concentrated in the Indian subcontinent and in countries to where numbers of Hindus migrated, such as the US, South Africa and the UK. It may not be common knowledge for non-believers, but Hinduism has several features which make it unique; there is no one perceived deity or prophet that is worshipped; there is not one set act of religious rites or performances. Rather than calling it a religion, some Hindus would prefer the term Dharma, as in India that is a broader term; by contrast, others would even describe themselves as atheist and that their perception is that Hinduism is more of a philosophy. That being said, there remains a sense of unity and a perception that there is more that unites believers than separates them. For example, a central tenet of Hinduism is that souls are immortal and the belief in rebirth and reincarnation. Death is therefore not seen as being the end – it is merely a natural process in the existence of a jiva, or being, and is seen as a time of resting and recuperating before moving on to the next stage of its journey. Each life on earth enables the jiva to learn from its past mistakes and inconsistencies, to overcome its blemishes, in the pursuit of becoming whole.

We cannot have likes and dislikes, preferences and prejudices, Hinduism teaches, and yet expect moksha, the liberation from the cycle of rebirth we are impelled to follow by the law of karma. As the holy book, the Bhagavad Gita, says, 'As a man casts off his worn-out clothes and takes on other new ones, so does the embodied soul cast off his worn-out bodies and enters other new.'

We in a sense therefore spend our time on Earth going through several cycles of learning to become better people – striving to become better, so that we may attain moksha.

Hindus believe that there is not so much a heaven and hell in the afterlife, more that there is no need to punish or reward, and the afterlife is there to remind the jiva of the true purpose of their experience. Once its learning is accomplished, it is reincarnated back on Earth to continue the samskara, or education.

So, in death, Hindus believe that by the very act of death, relatives of the deceased are in some way polluted, affected by it, until the soul completes the journey to the other world and the family are purified by funereal rituals.

Unless there is a compelling reason otherwise, the body is cremated as soon as is possible, often the same day. The body is placed upon the funeral pyre, and pyre lit. There is evidence as long ago as the 4th century BC of the tradition of Sati, or Suttee, where the wife of the deceased throws herself upon the pyre burning her dead husband. This practice was common until at least the mid-19th century, when the colonial British outlawed it in India.

I am sure there is a lot to take on board about key Hindu tenets; in that we are not the biggest thing in the world, and that the difficulties and trials of life – this life, what we know as life – are almost insignificant. It may seem that our life is great and wonderful and our bonds with the person who has died are such that we are grieving, and horribly so.

But Hinduism offers us a way to see that the life we know is only short-term and in the grand scheme, and in different forms, we all will be around for years.

Islam

There are two primary sects within Islam, and while Shia and Sunni differ on many aspects, there are some core areas they share. These include the belief there is another world that people enter after death, for which they prepare during their life on Earth.

If a person is thought to be near death, all the family are gathered and offer hope and kindness to the dying person, who is encouraged to say Shahada, the Muslim profession of faith that confirms there is no God but Allah.

Once the person has died, their eyes and lower jaw are covered with a clean sheet and mourners perform Dua, a prayer of supplication to Allah, asking Him to forgive the sins of the deceased.

The grave is dug perpendicular to Qiblah, the direction of Mecca, and the body is placed on its right hand side so it faces Mecca. Layers of wood and stone create a barrier to prevent direct contact of soil filling the grave and the body. In the funeral service, each mourner places three handfuls of soil. As they do so, they recite a prayer in Arabic, which roughly translates as, 'We created you from it [the earth], and return you to it, and will raise you from it a second time.'

It is acceptable in Islam to express grief over a death, and weeping at the time of death and at the funeral and burial are acceptable forms of expression. However, wailing and shrieking, the tearing of clothes or breaking of objects and expressing a lack of faith in Allah are all prohibited. It is considered important to remain dignified.

The grave is identified by only a small marker, as large monuments and decorations are prohibited. A period of mourning lasts for 40 days; however, widows are expected to mourn for four months and ten days.

Judaism

Life is valued above almost everything else, and the Jewish tradition teaches that all people are descended from a single person. As such, saving a single life is akin to saving the whole world and taking one life is like destroying the entire world.

Even in the most difficult of situations, the imminent and then actual loss of a loved one, the Torah holy book is there to strengthen, to guide and to help people grow and see beyond their loss.

Jewish people believe that death in this life leads to resurrection in the world to come and are encouraged to think about the dissolution of the bonds between the body and the soul. Just as the soul enters the body in stages – from conception, on to pregnancy and then birth – so to it often leaves the body in stages. Sight or hearing may weaken as a person gets older, but as long as there is life in the body the soul is present.

When death is close at hand, the person who is passing away, or someone close to them if they are unable, is encouraged to say the Shema, the prayer: 'Hear O Israel, the L-rd is our Gd, the L-rd is one.'

(Jewish people do not always use the full name for the deity they worship.)

These words are said at what is seen as the culmination of the person's life, when the sum total of his or her achievements is brought to fruition – when they are spiritually at their moment of the greatest potential.

A second important aspect of the process is Teshuvah, or a taking stock and confession of previous sins, shortcomings and failures, and seeks that G-d heals those failures and makes the person whole. Teshuvah can be achieved at any point in life, but at no time is it more opportune than when in life's closing moments.

According to the Talmud, the ancient holy text, the soul does not completely depart this world until after the burial (cremation is not allowed under Jewish law). There are quite complex mourning procedures in Judaism, which are characterised as gradually decreasing in intensity. Above all, the intention is to show respect to the dead and comfort to the living.

Immediately after the death, the body is covered and laid out, and candles are lit. The person is never left alone until after the burial, and no one must eat or drink in the presence of the dead – to do so would be insulting to the person who has died, as they can no longer do these things themselves.

The period after a person has died, and before their burial, is known as Aninut. During this initial stage, it is customary for the family of the deceased to tear their clothing – for a parent on the left side of the chest, above the notional heart; if it is another relative, the tear is made on the right side. Nowadays, it is commonplace to wear a ribbon with a symbolic rip in it – although for other people this is regarded as insufficient.

This Aninut typically lasts for only a couple of days – Judaism requires a quick burial – and the family are traditionally left alone to allow the full expression of grief. Condolence visits are not expected until after the burial, during the period of seven days known as Shiva, the traditional week of Jewish mourning. The family of the deceased gather at their house; they sit on low stools or on floor rather than on chairs, do not wear leather shoes, do not shave or cut their hair; wear make-up; go to work; and do not do things for comfort or pleasure – such as have a bath, have sex, put on fresh clothing or even study Torah, the religious texts, save for those verses that relate to death and mourning. Mourners wear the clothes they tore at the time of learning of the death, or wore to the funeral. Mirrors in the house are covered and prayer services are held in the house – for certain prayers friends, neighbours and relatives assist in making up the Minyan; the quorum of ten people required.

The next phase of mourning is called Shloshim, which last for thirty days, during which mourners do not attend celebrations, such as parties, and do not listen to music, cut their hair or shave.

After that, and lasting until twelve months after the death, is the period known as Avelut, which is observed only for a parent.

After that, the family only mourns the passing of their loved one on the anniversary of their death.

It is important to remember that the son of the deceased must, every day, for eleven months, stand up in front of a Minyan, a quorum of ten adult men, and recite a Kaddish, otherwise known as a mourner's prayer. Just when the mourner's faith might be most likely to be tested, they must stand up and reaffirm their commitment to G-d. To do so reflects upon the character of the person who has died – he has raised a son who will honour his parent by performing this task, someone who could express such faith in the face of personal loss.

I am sure the quite regimented set of rituals in Judaism can provide comfort and security for those who have been bereaved.

Navajo

Navajo customs and practices around death reflect the ancient traditions that they do not fear death, but rather, they fear that the dead will return to the living, or they will be exposed to evil spirits. The dead person is buried quickly, often with little ceremony.

Navajo people believe that when someone dies they go to the underworld and as such, every ritual is part of taking precautions that the dead person does not come back to the world of the living. As a result, Navajo are reluctant to look at a dead body and contact with a deceased person is restricted to only a few people.

When someone is dying, family members and the medicine man stay with the person until close to the end. Shortly before death, everyone except for one or two individuals will leave. Those who remain will be the closest relatives of the terminal person and the most willing to expose themselves to evil spirits.

There is always this fear that the dead person's spirit may return; historically the dead body is taken a long way north on a newly acquired horse. After the body is buried, the horse is slain and also buried, so that the dead person can ride it on to the new life.

If the person passes away at home, the dwelling is torn down and destroyed.

It is believed that the spirit can attach itself to a place, an object or a person if this important part of the process is interrupted. For the same reason, great care is taken so no footprints are left from the burial site, in case the departed spirit might follow the footprints back and attach itself to the person who made them.

According to traditional Navajo beliefs, birth, life and death are all part of an ongoing cycle. It is the natural course of things. As such, crying and outward demonstrations of grief are not usually seen when someone dies.

This should not be seen as a lack of caring; according to Navajo burial customs, the spirit's journey to the next world can be interrupted if too much emotion, too much upheaval, is shown.

It seems, perhaps to our eyes, as though death is something that people get through with the minimum of fuss – perhaps this is in part due to what historically appear to have been very tough lives. Perhaps the pressure to find food and to survive have in the past meant it was simply impractical to 'dwell' upon the loss. It is possible the belief system evolved to make it acceptable for people almost to get on with life again as quickly as possible. That is not any way seeking to demean the feelings and beliefs of the Navajo. What admirably tough people, who I cannot help but think have evolved a belief system that reflects the tough nature of their lives.

Sikhism

Sikhs believe the soul itself is not subject to death, as they believe in reincarnation, as a human or as an animal.

Sikhs believe that everything that happens is Hukam, or the will of Waheguru (God), and that there is a divine spark in each of us that is part of Waheguru. This spark is taken back to him when the person is finally released from the cycle of rebirth – called Mukti. There are 8,400,000 forms of life, and the soul can journey through several before they can reach Waheguru.

A key tenet is that only humans know the difference between right and wrong, so it is only after the soul's time on earth within a human being that the cycle can be broken. They therefore believe in karma, in that the actions and consequences of these actions decide whether a soul can be released from the cycle of rebirth.

Rather than lamenting the passing of an individual, Sikhism teaches resignation to the will of the creator, emphasising that death is a natural process and an opportunity for reunion of the soul with its maker.

As such, memorials are discouraged.

I hope that you have found this chapter on different religions as interesting to read as I found to research about. It made me realise that we know surprisingly little about religions that are different to the one we have grown up closest to.

I have tried to find passages that piqued my curiosity or that could prove interesting to others. I have tried to not get too bogged down and go into too intense detail, but instead to attempt to summarise and introduce sometimes quite difficult concepts and suggest possible, potential avenues for further reading.

I have at no time sought to consciously favour one religion above another or attempt to influence the reader to favour one religion above another.

I merely hope that your God, or indeed god or G-d go with you and help provide you with help, comfort and security. I am so sorry for your loss.

If there is anything I have written here that is in any way offensive to you, then please forgive me. My intention has here been, as it has been everywhere in this book, to write words merely in the hope of helping to provide comfort.

There may be other aspects that have no specific connection to any faith that you want to include in any funeral service. People often play music that meant something to the person who has died, or dress in a way that reflects one of their interests or hobbies. Funerals and wakes of course used to be solemn and serious affairs, but nowadays people often want to opt for more of a celebration of that person's life.

CHAPTER 10

Useful Information

Messages to Remember

1. People deal with things in their own way – grief is as personal as a fingerprint

2. Be kind to yourself. You cannot help the way you feel.

3. It is OK to feel angry and resentful, they are typical during this process

4. There is no right or wrong way to grieve, and no need to apologise

5. Do what feels comfortable for you

6. Be up front with people. You can ask for what it is you want, and say, 'Please can we talk about something else'; 'Ring me back in five minutes'; 'Please let me cry for a minute'; 'I cannot go to that event or do what you suggest, it will be too painful.'

7. You or the situation will never be 'better' or back to normal. You will just feel less broken and find a new kind of normal.

8. You will not stop loving that person, just because they are not there physically; you will just stop sharing your life with them as you had

9. Grief needs time, which might feel like a luxury – but it is not a luxury. It is a necessity, there is no timeframe.

10. There is no easy way to lose someone

11. There are no quick fixes or formulas to follow

12. Find your own way to celebrate and remember your loved one

13. Remember that you can never be fully prepared, and it is fine that you are not, or were not

14. Some days you will need to get through one at a time and, on really bad days, hour by hour and maybe even minute by minute

15. Go easy on yourself. Do not beat yourself up.

Further information and websites to consult.

Advice and support websites (All begin www.). Some may be homepages, but by searching 'bereavement' or 'grief' some useful information can be found

bereavement.co.uk

bereavementsupport.co.uk

nhs.uk

samaritans.org

macmillan.org.uk – Macmillan Cancer Support

cruse.org.uk – Cruse Bereavement Care

sueryder.org – Hospice and neurological care

mariecurie.org.uk – Care and support through terminal illness

priorygroup.com – Mental health group, counselling services

muchloved.com – Online tribute charity

supportline.org.uk – Confidential emotional support helpline

widowedandyoung.org.uk – WAY, charity support widowed and young people

thelossfoundation.org – Bereavement support charity

hospiceuk.org

mind.org.uk – Mental health charity

thelightbeyond.com

For children grieving over a lost parent:

winstonswish.org.uk

For parents and their families grieving over a lost child:

tcf.org.uk – The Compassionate Friends

lullabytrust.org.uk

uk-sands.org – The Stillbirth and Neonatal charity

For both:

childbereavementuk.org

Bereavement from suicide:

uk-sobs.org.uk

mind.org.uk

Discussion forums are quite common, but in particular:

forums.grieving.com

thelightbeyond.com

sueryder.org

Finding a counsellor:

bacp.co.uk

https://counsellorsuk.org

nhs.uk – search for counsellors

Books:

Dying to Be Me: My Journey from Cancer, to Near Death, to Near Healing by Anita Moorjani

Proof of Heaven: A Neurosurgeon's Journey into the Afterlife by Dr Eben Alexander

'You'll Get Over It': The Rage of Bereavement by Virginia Ironside

Local support

St. Albans bereavement network

Conclusion

During the course of this book, I have tried to talk about grief and bereavement, after finding out through personal experience that we do not talk about it – and that what we do end up talking about gets twisted and mixed up.

I have provided some information about helping a friend or someone close to you who is grieving, in the hope that you can become the person you want to be in helping them.

A chapter on religion was intended to provide possible avenues to explore in the hope of finding peace in one way or another.

I have also drawn on my experiences in the hope of providing suggestions here to help other people find their way through this horrible experience. I hope I have helped.

I would just like to add that, while in the middle of everything that is happening, it can be difficult to realise the extent of which you are suffering; when I was grieving soon after I was bereaved, I thought I was OK, and I wasn't. It was much worse and had affected me to a much greater and deeper extent than I had realised. I could only see that with distance.

What I have learned is that you will not go 'back to normal' because the normal that you knew has fundamentally changed. But there will be a 'new normal', and it will be OK when you get there.

Be kind to yourself and remember, you are stronger than you think.

You can tell people what it is that you want. There is no right or wrong way to grieve, it is you who is grieving, no one else. I would advise you to take small steps, and aim to feel a little less broken every day. And try not to let the new pain and heartache that you feel over a loved one eclipse the happy memories you have of them.

Good luck.

About the author

I have worked as a beauty therapist for 16 years, during which I spent a lot of my treatments 'counselling' my clients. The contact with people and attempting to help them, by making them look and feel good, were my favourite elements of the job.

When I hit the life-changing year which led to this book, I re-evaluated what I wanted from my life and decided that I wanted to change and start my own business.

Cuddle a Memory bears was an idea I had while up late one night in the week after Dad died. I wanted to keep one of his many sweatshirts from a hot air balloon event, and it broke my heart to think it would live in the bottom of my wardrobe, to be only taken out occasionally for comfort. I wanted to look at it all the time, to use the fabric somehow. So, I set about designing my own teddy bear, which is unique to us, where the fabric could form the body. I personally think in terms of size, shape and style, it is a fabulous-looking bear, and have found that other people have enjoyed having fabric from clothing that means something to them turned into a bear.

When making them, I spend time and carefully choose which bits of the garment will create the best effect and the very best bear, and as it is sewn together it takes on a personality of its own. Often, I have made them for family and friends, so I know personally the stories of the person the garment belonged to and feel they come out as the bear emerges.

I am a very creative person who loves all things craft-related. I also have created memory boxes for family and friends, a perfect box to store their family memorabilia, and am looking to set up workshops to assist others in doing the same.

During the process of writing this book and working with Raymond Aaron, I realised that I needed to return to a path I had explored earlier in my life and decided that I wanted to become a counsellor. Over the years, life events have taken me into counselling and I have gained a great deal from working with different therapists, and have always felt that providing a similar service to help others is something I wanted and needed to do.

Please contact me with any messages or enquires at carolyn@ cuddleamemorybook.com or find my Facebook page Cuddle a Memory book.

I look forward to hearing from you, thank you.

Hugs
Carolyn

Made in the USA
Lexington, KY
23 April 2018